# GEORGIA
## HIGH SCHOOL FOOTBALL

---

### PEACH STATE PIGSKIN HISTORY

## JON NELSON

Charleston    London

THE

History
PRESS

Published by The History Press
Charleston, SC 29403
www.historypress.net

Unless otherwise noted, all images are by the author.

First published 2011

Manufactured in the United States

ISBN 978.1.60949.295.3

Library of Congress Cataloging-in-Publication Data

Nelson, Jon.
Georgia high school football : Peach State pigskin history / Jon Nelson.
p. cm.
ISBN 978-1-60949-295-3
1. Football--Georgia--History. 2. High school football players--Georgia--History. I. Title.
GV959.52.G4N45 2011
796.332'6209758--dc23
2011026791

*For Dad, I love you and I miss you…*

# CONTENTS

# FOREWORD

When doing a historical evaluation of high school athletics, several things jump out at a person. The uniforms sure looked funny back then. The quality of the equipment is certainly better now. Players tended to play multiple sports back then, and the "school team" had a special place in the hearts and minds of the community. These differences inevitably lead to comparisons of the exploits of the players and coaches in the different eras, and that sparks many debates.

The best thing to do, however, is to view high school athletics within the historical context in which they occurred. That way, a person can appreciate all the contributions made by players and coaches throughout Georgia over a number of years. Jon Nelson is a person who has an appreciation for the diverse aspects of high school athletics in Georgia, and his writings enable us to expand our appreciation of high school athletics as well.

Dr. Ralph Swearngin
Executive Director, Georgia High School Association

# ACKNOWLEDGEMENTS

If I listed every person who helped make this book possible, I would certainly, go over the forty-thousand-word limit given to me for this round. First, the obvious thanks go to Jessica Berzon and everyone at The History Press for pushing the idea and giving me the pleasure and privilege to make this happen. Everyone across this state of Football Fridays who has helped out with outright education, provided an interview, advice, photographs to help tell their own stories, talked me through their region and associated stories or proofread this manuscript to make sure everything is right, I can't thank all of you enough.

To my family—blood or otherwise—I can't thank you enough for your emotional support. To the rest of the Outlaws—your calls are always treasured. To my mom—I love you and thanks for the mindset of an English major. To my dad—I know you're watching.

Last, and certainly not least, to Patty, who puts up with me and my Fridays, I am blessed to have you as the love of my life.

# Chapter 1
## THE BEGINNING OF IT ALL

## IT ALMOST NEVER HAPPENED

The state of Georgia can thank the mother of Vonalbade "Von" Gammon for having any kind of football. Period.

Von Gammon was a college player for the University of Georgia who died while playing a game against the University of Virginia in 1897. As a result, the Georgia House of Representatives passed a resolution the next day to ban football by a vote of 91 to 3. The three college schools that played the sport at the time—Georgia, Georgia Tech and Mercer—all voluntarily disbanded their squads. The Georgia Senate followed with a vote outlawing football a few weeks later by a 31 to 4 margin. All Georgia governor William Atkinson needed to do was sign the resolutions into law, and football in the state would not exist.

Von Gammon's mother, Rosalind Burns Gammon, knowing what was transpiring in Atlanta, wrote a letter to her local representative that said in part:

> *His* [Gammon's] *interest in all manly sports, without which he deemed the highest type of manhood impossible, is well known by his classmates and friends, and it would be inexpressibly sad to have the cause he held so dear injured by his sacrifice. Grant me the right to request that my boy's death should not be used to defeat the most cherished object of his life.*

When Governor Atkinson was made aware of the letter and Mrs. Gammon's feelings on the matter, he didn't sign the resolution, and the movement to ban football in Georgia ended.

## THE ABSOLUTE BEGINNINGS

High schools, as we know them, started their existence in the late nineteenth century. Cedartown High School in northwest Georgia, as an example, dates its start to 1887. Community games took place in some organized settings in south Georgia towns like Thomasville and Valdosta as far back as 1895. But the sport of football started organized play in the early 1900s. Cedartown's Bulldogs date back to 1903, and other schools dotted around the state share the same timeline. You can even see a restored version of the team photo at Cedartown High School these days—with all eleven players—and the homage the 2003 team gave on the centennial anniversary in its reproductive photograph using current seniors.

Albany High School, Glynn Academy in Brunswick, Waycross High School (which would later turn into Ware County High School), Fitzgerald, Moultrie, Gainesville and Thomasville all started within that first decade in south Georgia, but two Savannah schools have one of the longest-standing rivalries in all of high school football in the United States.

One of the oldest recorded images of what would become high school football in the state of Georgia. Thomasville in 1895. *Courtesy TvilleBulldogs.com via Thomas County Museum of History.*

The 1903 Cedartown High Bulldogs. The restored picture hangs at Cedartown High School.

The private school (or "the Catholics")—Benedictine Military Academy (the last "E" is silent, by the way)—and the public school (or the "Crackers")—Savannah High—started playing in 1903 and have played 109 times since, including playoff games. The Benedictine Cadets lead the series 54-47-8, and the lone win for Benedictine in 2010 was against the Savannah High Blue Jackets for school win number 500. The first game in the series was played at the Bolton Street Athletic Park in front of a reported crowd of eight hundred. From 1920 to 1959, the game was played on Thanksgiving Day at Municipal Stadium to an overflow crowd. The next season, the teams began playing the game before Thanksgiving at the newly constructed Memorial Stadium.

"People had the [Thanksgiving Day] parade downtown and the [BC] guys would all march in their military uniforms into the stadium," 1985 graduate and current Benedictine head coach Mark Stroud told the *Savannah Morning News*'s Noell Barnidge. "People dressed up for the game. Everybody had dates. It was pretty cool. It really was. Afterward, the winning team would take a coffin decorated up and they would burn it on Broughton Street. Can you imagine anybody doing that now?"

Savannah and Benedictine, the oldest rivalry in the state. *Courtesy Maurice Sheppard.*

And the rivalry even had its own time on the Savannah city streets. *Courtesy Maurice Sheppard.*

Sometimes there would even be an effigy of a player inside the coffin, and students and fans from both schools would be present for the burning. The game was "the biggest event in Savannah until Georgia high school rule changes resulted in the game being played before Thanksgiving," says Maurice "Mutt" Sheppard, a 1959 Benedictine grad who wrote a book on the rivalry, *Savannah's Thanksgiving Day Football Classic: Benedictine Vs. Savannah High*.

"You got involved in that game from the time you were a youngster in grammar school," Albert "Whitey" Moore, a Savannah High grad, admitted to *Georgia Trend Magazine*'s Jerry Grillo. "Kids around town would ask one another which team you were for and you'd better get the answer right, depending on who was talking."

Whitey Moore would know what the Cadets–Blue Jackets game means to the town. He played for Savannah High, but his three brothers went to Benedictine.

## But Do We Really Want a League?

The November 4, 1911 edition of the *Atlanta Georgian and News* newspaper ran an editorial in the "Not News, But Views" section by Percy H. Whiting that proclaimed an Atlanta Prep League Athletic Association for high school football would be a bad idea. Whiting claimed that one school, Marist, didn't have a team at the time. Tech High couldn't field one, either. So that would leave only three schools with a chance at playing a season of football with one another—Boys' High, Georgia Military Academy and Peacock High. The opinion didn't stop there:

> It has long been known that football isn't a game that adapts itself to play through a league season. The experiment was made years ago and the failure was suggestive.
>
> The local prep association would do well to leave football leagues alone. If the individual teams want to play, that's well and good. But it is ridiculous to talk of a series of games for a championship.
>
> We still believe, as we long have, that the Prep league ought to take up soccer football as its Fall game. Certainly it will never do anything with American college football.

So much for listening to Whiting…

# THE FIRST STATE TITLES

As a rule, during the years of the North Georgia Interscholastic Athletic Association (1904–19) and the subsequent Georgia Interscholastic Athletic Association (1920–24), titles were "claimed" more than assigned or won, as they are today, complete with trophies and ceremonies on television. In the city of Atlanta, the *Constitution* newspaper claimed a champion—much to the chagrin of teams that thought themselves to be the best in any given year. But since the best teams may not have played one another in a fall schedule, the arbitration was indeed arbitrary. Some examples:

From 1907 to 1909 at Gordon High, Bob McWhorter ruled the grass as a halfback for the school. Gordon claimed a title in his senior year after a 60–0 win over Riverside High School.

In Tifton, the Tifton Agricultural and Mechanical School was an active squad in the 1910s. In 1915, the Aggies claimed the South Georgia Championship, beating Valdosta 33–0. A rivalry developed between Tifton A&M and Norman College, and the 1916 Aggies claimed that year's state title after winning the South Georgia Prep Association's championship game over Norman, 26–0.

Thomasville High's Bulldogs started in 1914 and, as was the case with a lot of teams in the era, either scored a lot of points or gave up a lot of points. The Bulldogs' first game ever was against Ochlocknee, and they put 55 points on the scoreboard in a win, but the next game against Valdosta was one where they gave up 66 in a loss. There would be titles in 1925 and 1927 for Head Coach James K. Harper. The South Georgia Athletic Association recognized the Bulldogs as their champs in two undefeated years.

Valdosta High started in 1914, and can you guess the number of people who showed up for the Wildcats' debut? Two—one athlete's parents.

A lot of Georgia schools that were just gaining momentum in the sport called for breaks during 1917 and 1918 due to World War I. Programs like the Fitzgerald Purple Hurricane, which may have played some kind of organized ball before the First World War, actually started their programs in 1919. Colquitt County High School, known as Moultrie High when it started, had played for five seasons before Harold Saxon's team went 7-0 and was named the South Georgia Champs. They would add another south Georgia title in 1928 under Dode Phillips in a season that included a scoreless tie against legendary Boys' High.

LaGrange High in western Georgia played a handful of games (as the records indicate) from its beginning in 1908 through the 1918 season—winning only three times, losing eleven and tying one. Bernie Moore would coach the team from 1918 to 1920 before he moved on to LSU and a tour as commissioner of the SEC. But the mid-1920s gave the then–LaGrange Veterans four "claimed" state titles under T.W. (Tatum) Gressette. LaGrange won thirty-one straight at one point and has titles from 1924 to 1926. They even organized a state championship game against Moultrie High on Thanksgiving Day 1926 to put all "claims" to rest that year.

The Lincoln County/Lincolnton High program started in 1922, and another rivalry began with its western neighbors in Wilkes County. W.T. Dunaway would take his first team to a 6-2-1 record—his first of five winning seasons in the school's first six years of play. But playing Washington High twice in 1922 only gave the then-Bearcats a 7–7 tie and a 13–6 loss against the neighboring Bearcats. Robert "Skeet" Willingham has written a book on what is now called Washington–Wilkes Tigers football and referred to game two in the series this way: "Though holding things in order on the field, the activities of the spectators could not be controlled and, because of unruly fan behavior, the two teams would not re-institute playing each other until 1939."

There had almost been another year in between during which the two played—1925. Wilkes County had won the East Georgia Championship, and Lincoln County wanted its piece of a championship in what would be called a "plus one" game in the present day after an 8-0-1 season. Wilkes declined the offer, and naturally, Lincolnton declared themselves to be the champions. The champions of exactly what, no one can actually figure out.

## The Next Step

In 1920, the Georgia Interscholastic Athletic Association (GIAA) was formed at the encouragement of Atlanta Boys' High principal W.O. Cheney. The member schools—Boys', Atlanta Tech, Lanier, Monroe A&M, Gordon, Georgia Military College (Milledgeville) and Riverside—tried to take care of a larger issue other than naming a champion. Since player eligibility was somewhat shady in some instances in the past, these schools wanted to try to have a way to make sure paperwork was available on each participating athlete, or if there was no proof, any athlete under the age of twenty had to sit out a year if he was transferring from one member school to another.

But the 1922 GMC squad had other ideas. After they lost a player to a car accident, *Atlanta Constitution* scribe Craddock Goins saw something he didn't like. According to the Georgia High School Football Historians Association, Goins wrote:

> *The Milledgeville institution is not interested in the GIAA, but out to give its students all the football amusement they want and to try to turn out winning teams…it is high time the schools of the state get together and see just how each one stands on the matter of athletic control. If the GIAA, then they should observe its rules, for Georgia wants to call some team "champion."*

Another unique idea the GIAA brought about after the GMC incident was the implementation of an impartial arbiter to determine eligibility of athletes and just who the champions would be at the end of the year. The arbiter also was responsible for the first North-South title game starting in 1925. But that wouldn't be the end of it by any means…

## SMITHIES AND PURPLE HURRICANES

As the only two high schools inside the city of Atlanta, Tech High and Boys' High garnered a majority of the attention in the time of the GIAA. The two schools combined for thirteen titles from 1923 to 1945 and were the pipelines for most of the talent that went to play college ball at the well-known schools in the Southeast. Claude "Gabe" Tolbert was the head coach for the Tech High Smithies' first two titles, in 1924 and 1928. Tech High would add crowns in 1933 and 1937 as both schools created their own who's who for talent pools at games played on Fridays at Ponce de Leon Park—the home of the minor league Atlanta Crackers.

For Tech, Johnny "Stumpy" Thomason was a key fullback for the '24 title, and Norman "Buster" Mott, Bill Hutt and Heavy Hammond were the backfield for the 1928 team.

R.L. "Shorty" Doyal was the head coach for the rival Boys' Purple Hurricanes squad from 1925 to 1946 that won nine championships: 1932, 1934, 1935, 1939, 1940, 1941, 1943, 1944 and 1945. Doyal had the likes of end George Roberts, quarterback Billy Mims, halfback Lawrence Hayes and center Charles Furchgott to get fans' appetites whetted until Clint Castleberry ran roughshod from 1939 to 1941 and took three straight titles. Castleberry was rated one of the top high school players in the state's history and continued his success at Georgia Tech in the 1940s.

Shorty even had his son, "Buck," at center for the 'Canes second three-peat from 1943 to 1945 as they won six of seven titles. Doyal's fullback for those last three titles was an athlete named Porter Payne. His son, William, is better known to this generation as Billy Payne—the man credited with bringing the Summer Olympics to Atlanta in 1996. Payne and Ewell Pope, a six-foot, 160-pound guard, blocked for Castleberry. Doyal even said of Castleberry, "He was so good I had to take him out of the games to hold the score down."

For the 1945 game, regarded by some as the best matchup of all time in Georgia high school history, a record crowd of twenty-five thousand gathered at Ponce de Leon Park, the home of the Atlanta Crackers, and another seven thousand were turned away at the gates. Boys' had won five of the past six state titles, and Tech was 9-0 with its best team in years. Boys' won 14–0 on touchdown runs by Porter Payne to get the GIAA title for the ninth and final time.

The two schools were even housed in the same building, which is currently the grounds for Grady High School and Stadium. Each school had its own wooden portable annexes—one on one end of the property and one at the other end. The football teams practiced at the same time and at the same place—Piedmont Park, which was across the street. Boys' High practiced on the south end and Tech High worked out on the north end. The fields were on the west end of the Park, opposite Fourteenth Street.

In the last years of the GIAA, Tech High came back for an undefeated season in 1946. Pierce McWhorter starred at halfback alongside Bobby North and Sid Williams, the future founder of Life University in the Atlanta suburb of Marietta.

The Boys'-Tech game would, over time, be the matchup that would decide the state title, as Coach Doyal would become disenchanted with the idea that if his North Division team had a better record (including head-to-head) with his South Division counterpart, he would still have to play them all over again for a championship. Before the 1935 season, he was able to get a rule passed allowing that if that situation came to be as the

Grady High School today.

end of the season drew near, the divisional playoff was waived. Odds are that Boys' High would then get the title.

Boys' and Tech were eventually merged to form Grady High School. With all the titles these schools won, one school may have the right to call "Scoreboard"—even as Tech held the edge in the series 18 wins to 15 (or, in other record books, this mythical series ended as an 18-18-1 tie). The series finale was played at Grant Field on the Georgia Tech campus in front of a reported crowd of twenty-three thousand.

As a side note, LaGrange may be the only team in Georgia High School Association (GHSA) history with an all-time winning record against Boys' High. The Veterans were 3-0-1 in four meetings—winning in 1922 (44–0), 1924 (14–0) and 1925 (20–6) and tying in 1939 with Boys' B team at 6–6.

## OUTSIDE THE CITY

Conference titles have been "claimed" around the state of Georgia ever since schools resumed play after World War I in one form or another. Smaller schools went as far as starting their own classification and championship designations as a group in 1930 with the North Georgia Interscholastic Conference (NGIC) and the South Georgia Football Association (SGFA). If you were in towns like Sylvester, Camilla and Blakely, your home was the Southwest Georgia Group (SGG).

Valdosta High started its run as a national powerhouse by winning a North-South playoff against Clarke Central in 1920 and winning other region titles in 1923, 1924, 1927 and 1938. The first of the Wildcats' twenty-two state titles came in 1940 after a two-game playoff run against Newt "Badman" Godfree's Tift County team and Cedartown's Bulldogs in front of a crowd of 1,500. After the semifinal win, a story goes that Godfree didn't even finish the season as a teacher and a coach, quitting his job and leaving town, never to be heard from again.

Billy Grant, Bubba Tillman and Sonny Stephenson (the receiver whom Head Coach Wright Bazemore regarded as the "best pass receiver we've ever had") were a dangerous grouping as the 'Cats won their second title seven years later in Class B. The Fitzgerald High legend (and one-time *Ripley's Believe It or Not* feature for being the best high school athlete in the country) was the head coach for that squad as they knocked off Albany and Gainesville. The Red Elephants, however, still claim a co-champion title from that same year as NGIC champs. Bazemore actually was the head coach for the Valdosta basketball, tennis and golf teams. All four won state titles in 1947 and 1948. His philosophy was: "We're not going to give 100 percent. We're going to give 110 percent, or we're not going to play."

By 1937, a system had been created for a Class B title game. Spalding County High (Griffin) won the first Class B title in 1937, finishing 9-0-1 after defeating Grant Gillis's Moultrie High, the SGFA representative, 6–0. Harold McNabb's Albany High team won a Class B title in 1939, followed by one in 1943 against Griffin as Weyman Sellers's name was etched in Dougherty County history books with a game-winning touchdown catch.

Thomasville would return in 1941 and 1945 as champs. The '41 squad, coached by E.O. Garner, had five teams shut out on their way to a south Georgia title win against Valdosta. Their state title dreams came to a close with an 18–0 shutout loss to Athens High in Albany. Garner's 9-1-1 team won both south Georgia and Class B state titles four years later with wins over Cairo and Cedartown. The Bulldogs were 2-0-1 against the Syrupmakers that year and claimed Thomas County's first football crown in the process.

Class B title games would go until 1947, when the Georgia High School Association was formed, and the SGFA and Class B games were almost always played in Albany.

Chapter 2

# THE FORTIES AND FIFTIES

The Poets of Lanier High were the first team to make their mark in the GHSA era with back-to-back titles in 1947 and 1948. And for the Poets, in their career before the high school was dissolved by 1970, the seasons seemed to be feast or famine. A semifinals loss in 1949 and a finals loss in 1950 were followed by a 2-8 season in 1951 under Head Coach Selby Buck. The team rebounded by 1953, only to lose to Grady High of Atlanta in the finals and hover around .500 for the remainder of the school's run. Two quarterfinal losses to Valdosta in 1968 and 1969 would symbolize the end for one of the state's comet-like performances for high school football.

## THE FABULOUS PHANTOM OF FITZGERALD

James "Lauren" Hargrove did everything for the Fitzgerald Purple Hurricane—offense, defense, kicking game, punt return—in the 1948 title game against Decatur. He showed all of it off for Fitzgerald's only state title ever over Decatur.

After spotting Decatur a 13-0 lead, Hargrove scored two touchdowns and kicked what would be the winning extra point in a 20–19 final. That year, the state's first all-American was the most sought-after football player in the nation according to Gene Asher in his book *Legends—Georgians Who Lived Impossible Dreams*. According to Asher, Hargrove finished his career with 450 points—in three seasons.

John Wiggins, secretary-treasurer of the Fitzgerald booster club for forty-two consecutive years, told Rick Badie of the *Atlanta Journal-Constitution* in 2009 that Hargrove was the "Herschel Walker of his day." Wiggins also told Badie about just how fast Hargrove was in his high school and college years: "He remembered a race the Atlanta Crackers had at one of its baseball games. Four of the state's fastest running backs competed in the 100-yard dash with cleats and helmets. 'Lauren walked away from all of them,' Mr. Wiggins said. 'He was a natural.'"

Hargrove went on to the University of Georgia and was set to become part of the Green Bay Packers after graduating. But his induction into the army for World War II came first. After his service, he found out that the Pack had traded his rights. Hargrove decided he wasn't going to play for his new team, so he retired from football right then and there.

Alongside Wright Bazemore, no one is revered more than Hargrove in the eyes of Purple Hurricane fans everywhere.

## PUTTING ON THE BRAKES

Morgan County finished out the decade with a run of its own in Class B—four titles in the last five seasons for Head Coach Charlie Brake. In 1955, twin brothers and twin halfbacks Roy and Toy Sims led the Bulldogs to a win over Vidalia in Sandersville 21–12. The back to back was completed in '56 when Blakely-Union fell to the team led by first-year Head Coach Bill Corry 13–7. Blakely-Union had won 21 of its last 22 going in to the game, which was held in Thomaston as a neutral site this time around.

Two years later, Corry had his second chance after beating Mitchell County in Fort Valley 20–7. The Bulldogs had lost their season opener to Rockdale County but then reeled off twelve straight for the title behind. Jake "Snooks" Saye, who had been part of the first three crowns, would end up in Athens and continue his career at the University of Georgia. Oddly enough, Morgan County started the 1959 season ranked number two behind Blakely-Union again, but Corry and the Bulldogs would wrap up their fourth title in the five years with a 7–0 squeaker over Brooks County in another title game in Fort Valley. The team would be the only undefeated team in the final Roberts Rankings for the season, but there is a discrepancy as to whether the team won 13 times or 14—8 of them by shutout.

The twin McWhorter brothers, Bob and Bill, would give Corry a fourth title in 1962 as the Bulldogs started their year with five straight shutouts and took care of Hawkinsville in week fourteen. Corry would not be a head coach another season, and he wrapped up his career 78-6-3—a winning percentage of .914—never losing more than twice in a row.

The deepest any Morgan County team has played in a season since was 1990, when the Bulldogs were in the quarterfinals.

## THE BEGINNINGS OF "THE BAZE" AND WINNERSVILLE

Valdosta's dominance as a state power began here: seven regional titles, six south Georgia titles and five state titles in a seven-year period—three in a row from 1951 to 1953 and back-to-back titles in 1956 and 1957. The region title in 1950 was a quiet announcement that the Wildcats would not be stopped in their quest for superiority. The year 1951 had two playoff wins for a state title, but 1952 was known for eight shutouts—including the 30–0 state title game win against LaGrange. After the win, Coach Bazemore was given a television, a watch and a shotgun for his efforts. The Wildcats never scored fewer than 26 points in any win and never gave up more than 7 until an extra playoff game played in Columbus, Georgia, the week after the state championship.

The Wildcats played in the Peanut Bowl against West Springfield High School out of Massachusetts, so you could say it took playing an out-of-state school for someone to score into double digits. It was still a 28–26 win for the home team. The game in Columbus served, in some circles, as the "national championship game" for high school football. Others treated it as an exhibition and an extra game on the schedule around New Year's Day.

Bazemore switched to the two-platoon system around the '52 season, and his offense went from the single-wing to the T formation and even the spread formation. One play, the "Center Keep," which in the modern day would be called something of a "Fumblerooskie" play, even seemed to work for him—until it was outlawed.

In 1953, the Wildcats weren't even ranked number one as defending champ and were only third as late as week nine when a win over Jesup High finally put the team on top. The only blemish on the score sheet was a tie with Moultrie High as, for the second year in a row, LaGrange was beaten for the state title 48–7. The Grangers had a 7–0 lead before the 'Cats scored 48 unanswered. Bobby Renfroe was the star tailback for the squad coming in, but he was out for most of the year with a broken arm. He would come back for the LaGrange game and score twice as the team would finish top

The look you never want from Wright Bazemore. *Courtesy Valdosta Wildcats Museum.*

ranked and 12-0-1. Montgomery Bell High from Tennessee was the Peanut Bowl opponent and came out a 24–0 loser.

Bazemore's team won an electricity-shortened Class AA title game in 1956. Johnny Welch and Ben Smith led the ground game that would make their way to a title game against Druid Hills in Valdosta. Up 27–0 with 3:36 left in the game, the lights over Cleveland Field went out. The officials, both on the field and at the stadium, were scrambling for an hour to try to fix the problem, but no solution could be figured out, and the game was called.

Quarterback Dale Williams was knocked out of the semifinal game against Thomasville in 1957 with a kidney injury as the Wildcats were going for the back to back. Coach Bazemore put halfback Bozey Thomas in his place for the final against 1950 champ Rockmart. The Yellow Jackets scored first and gave the Wildcats their second deficit for the entire year. Thomas scored twice from that moment on, and title five for the '50s stayed at Cleveland Field (13–7) and the 'Cats wrapped up the year an undefeated 13-0.

David Waller—Valdosta Wildcats Museum curator, longtime Touchdown Club member and close personal friend of Bazemore—admits:

*People would always wonder what Coach Bazemore would say when we'd be down at the half, and then we'd come out blowing everybody's doors off in the second half. Truth is: he didn't say anything. They were always prepared for the games during the week. There wasn't any need to tell you what you were doing wrong. You just weren't playing up to the capabilities you had.*

*He would shame you...just walking around saying, "Mmm...mmm... mmm."* [Waller moves his bowed head from side to side.] *And just before the halftime was over, he would say, "Your mommas and daddies are right there in the stands. Your grandmammas and your granddaddies." And they were mostly in those days. "Your brothers, sisters, uncles and your aunts are all out there...I'd be ashamed to call myself a Wildcat." That's all he said. He didn't go over anything because that wasn't how he trained you. He had you ready and so you came out thinking that you wanted to show them and 99 out of 100 times, if you were behind you came from behind to win 'cause that's just the way it was.*

# A Coach's Show? For a High School?

Frank Inman was a successful high school coach in Augusta for the Academy of Richmond County (ARC) from 1956 to 1961, winning a state title in his first season as head of the Musketeers and being at the forefront of one of the most successful coaching runs in a single season in high school history. ARC won the state title in four boys' sports: track, football, baseball and golf. Inman was the head coach of that golf squad and made it to the state title game in two other sports—tennis and basketball—as head coach.

But it was the football team that drew visitors from all over—especially if you wanted to see game film. Inman co-hosted a coaches' show on WRDW-TV early on Sunday afternoons that actually bumped Wally Butts's Georgia Bulldog show from its time slot. It was years ahead of its time and looked like most every coaches' show seen on the air today.

Matt Middleton broke down the trailblazing experience in September 2009 for the *Augusta Chronicle*:

*Opposing coaches, legend has it, used to come into the area on Sundays and check into a motel and watch the show for scouting purposes. The show was the first of its kind among high school coaches,* [co-host Lee] *Sheridan said, one of several areas in which Inman was considered an innovator.*

*"He was ahead of his time in many areas…during a golden era of Richmond Academy athletics," said Sheridan.*

*His detailed scouting reports and feel for the game always made them feel more prepared than their opponent. It was part of their weekly schedule to meet their coach after his Sunday television show.*

*Inman would pull out a 16-millimeter roll from the television studio, and they would go over game film together, a pioneering process.*

*His memory of opponents stretched beyond the film he gathered. Preparing for a game against Savannah, Inman once pulled a player aside and detailed how their opponent would surprise them with a quick-kick, a third-down punt.*

*He had seen it years ago, and their formation was the tell. The Musketeers ended up blocking a quick-kick attempt that game, returning it for a touchdown.*

*"I remember it only because it happened exactly like he said it would," said Dr. Randy Smith, who played for Inman from 1959–61.*

Inman left ARC after the 1961 season to be an assistant for both Johnny Griffith and Vince Dooley in Athens at the University of Georgia. That last class had nine NCAA Division I signees—a number thought to be a GHSA record at the time. Inman's coaching style and skills rubbed off on one of his charges from that 1956 team. Legendary Auburn head coach Pat Dye was regarded as the star of the Musketeers at the time and said about Inman, "He was a great coach, but a better man. He touched all our lives."

And television can thank Frank Inman being light years ahead of the rest for his ideas in promotion of a program that a lot of schools do today—not to mention the reviewing of game film for previewing the next opponent on your schedule with your own players to stay ahead of the curve. Which Inman certainly was.

# A Devil of a Coach

Bobby Gentry was in Athens, Georgia, where he got his first taste of football as a manager for Red Maddox at Athens (later Clarke Central) High School. He quarterbacked Coach Alex McCaskill's single-wing offense of the 1940s. During the week following Pearl Harbor in 1941, his Athens High team won the state championship in a game against Thomasville. He

*Left*: Bobby Gentry, the coach who first brought titles to Hawkinsville. *Courtesy Sam Crenshaw.*

*Below*: The fifty-year reunion of the first champs in Hawkinsville. *Courtesy Sam Crenshaw.*

was also a member of the state boys' basketball championship team later that same school year.

After his time in the U.S. Army Air Corps, he returned to be an assistant for a few years before one of his former coaches, Eddie Harrell, became superintendent of schools in Hawkinsville in 1947. Hawkinsville had just restarted its football program, and Harrell contacted Gentry to be the new head coach.

Hawkinsville had its first unbeaten regular season in 1952, only to lose in the first round of the playoffs. In 1953, Gentry led Hawkinsville to its first-ever state championship with an unbeaten and untied record, knocking off Calhoun in the final 27–6 behind the running of Melvin Borum. In 1954, the Devils went back to back, only giving up 52 points in 12 games total and beating Buford in the title game. Coach Gentry was named Coach of the Year in 1959 after his third title came in a victory over North Cobb. His last title appearance came in 1962, but he was the Red Devils coach for twenty-nine seasons—wrapping with a record of 203-96-10. Coach Gentry was elected to the Georgia Athletic Coaches Association Hall of Fame on June 4, 2005, before dying in December of that year.

But the thought in central Georgia is that Gentry's greatest victory may have come as he was at the forefront of integrating Pulaski County's public schools during the 1960s. He even returned to become the county school superintendent before retiring altogether. His retirement years were spent watching his Red Devils from a chair on the practice field; he and his family would see the successes of the team return decades later.

# HE'S A HAUSS

"In the 1950s, if you were a boy, you almost had to play football," Len Hauss said. "You were almost a traitor to your school if you didn't play."

Hauss rushed for over 1,500 yards with fifteen touchdowns as a senior fullback at Jesup (now Wayne County) High. In 1959, he helped lead the Yellow Jackets to a record of 11-2 and the Class AA state championship—a 35–7 win over Rossville.

The following is from the *Jesup Sentinel*, Thursday, December 17, 1959:

> *Len Hauss, magnificent all season, closed out his career in brilliant fashion Friday night while leading the Jesup High Yellow Jackets to a 35–7 rout of Rossville High in the Georgia Class AA championship football game. Hauss, a 6-1, 220-pound fullback, termed by Coach Donaldson as one of the best backs of his coaching career, and who signed a grant-in-aid contract with the University of Georgia on Saturday morning, treated some 5,000 fans at Jaycee Stadium to a great show. He scored three touchdowns, recovered two fumbles to set up others, gained 145 yards on 22 carried for a 6.6 average and was a standout as linebacker as the Jacket defensive unit completely stymied Rossville.*

"We beat the Waycross Bulldogs for the region championship, the Thomasville Bulldogs for South Georgia championship and the Rossville Bulldogs for state championship," he told *In the Game Magazine*'s John

DuPont in 2010. "Then I became a Georgia Bulldog." How's that for irony?

Auburn, Georgia and Georgia Tech were all in the bidding for Hauss out of high school. Georgia assistant coach J.B. "Ears" Whitworth won over Bobby Dodd and Shug Jordan for the four-year trip to Athens. "My mother thought that Coach Whit would look after her baby because Athens was big time compared to Jesup at that time," Hauss said.

Hauss went on to a successful fourteen-year NFL career that would even give the big lineman the chance to be the head of the National Football League Players' Association (NFLPA). He has been enshrined in the Wayne County Sports Hall of Fame and the Georgia Sports Hall of Fame, and he was also named one of the Seventy Greatest Redskins of All Time to mark the team's seventieth anniversary back in 2002.

"Not a whole lot of ballplayers were able to go to college if they didn't play ball," he told DuPont. "Chances are if you were from Jesup, you didn't have any other way to go."

## Northwest Georgia Shines

The AA Rossville Bulldogs went two for three in title games, winning two in a row in 1954 and 1955 under Glenn Wade. The '54 title was an outright championship over Savannah High, and the second was a 13–13 tie with LaGrange at Barron Stadium in Rome, Georgia—something of a geographical midpoint. The Class B Model Blue Devils would also go back to back in '53 and '54 under Coach N.S. Woodard, but both schools would rarely see those same kinds of successes as they moved forward. Before Rossville changed over in 1989, Frank Fabris coached the navy blue and white to a fantastic run: a finals loss in 1959, a semifinals loss in 1960, a finals loss to Waycross in 1961 and a title in 1962. But the school would only have one ten-win season after that in the next twenty-six seasons. Model would have one other championship year, a 15-0 campaign under Wayne Huntley in 1979, but they haven't had any other double-digit win seasons since.

Another shining star came from Monticello, in central Georgia, as the Hurricanes had back-to-back seasons of their own in 1955 and 1956—under two different head coaches, Milton McLaney and Bobby Holland. The 'Canes actually carried a thirty-two-game unbeaten streak into the 1957 title game against Waynesboro High in Burke County. But after that run of success, the highest win total at the school has been eleven—achieved three times in the late 1980s and early 1990s.

# FRAN THE MAN

Part of the gap in Valdosta's championships in Class A in the mid-1950s can go to the Athens High Trojans. After Weyman Sellers's team lost in the semifinals to Rockmart in 1954, they came back to win the '55 title over Bazemore and the Wildcats.

Their quarterback at the time? Junior Francis Asbury Tarkenton. His father wanted to pursue a doctorate at the University of Georgia, so the family moved from Washington, D.C., to Athens when Tarkenton was eleven. And Fran already had that one element that would make him famous as a quarterback throughout his career: elusiveness.

"We played touch football every day," Tarkenton told Steve Hannon of the *Athens Banner-Herald*, "and you had to be elusive because the alleys were narrow and you didn't have much room to dodge." Tarkenton would go on to be an all-state talent as a senior in football, baseball and track as a senior—for a team that went 4-5-1.

# Chapter 3

# THE STREAKIN' SIXTIES

## CARROLLTON'S CHARLIE GRISHAM

"He was crazy enough to offer me a job, and I was crazy enough to take it." That was how Charlie Grisham described Carrollton city school superintendent F.M. Chalker's pitch to hire an inexperienced coach for an opening—all for $3,400 a year under Hugh Maddox. He was the backfields coach for the 1956 squad that would tie Statesboro for a state title, and when Maddox went upstairs to become principal, the assistant was now in charge.

Over the course of the next twenty-nine years, he amassed a 261-69-13 record plowing through Class A for most of the 1960s and the early part of the '70s, finishing with sixteen region titles, including ten in a row from 1959 to 1968 and another six in a row from 1970 to 1976. There would be eight North Georgia titles, an induction into the Georgia State Athletic Hall of Fame, a National Coach of the Year award in 1982 and a large place reserved in the history of high school football.

When Charlie Grisham coached his first game for the Trojans in 1958, he used a T-formation offense. Everyone else ran fancier things, but for Carrollton, it would always be the Notre Dame box. J.R. Porch coached Grisham in the town of Verbena, Alabama, which Porch referred to as the "end of the trail." The Verbena teams had won fifty-one in a row using that offense, so it's easy to see how Grisham was influenced and knew what worked.

"All we care about is getting across the goal line," Grisham admitted years later. "We don't emphasize individual statistics and we try to let all of our players get in the game." That mindset worked for those three decades he was in charge. "My old high school coach—he was thirty-eight years old back in '47—he said, 'Hell, anybody can run the ball as long as you block a hole in there. If you make a hole, my mama can run the ball.' I agree with most of that. But I was a running back in high school and college, and I do believe I was a little faster than my mama."

Grisham had graduated, by his count, eighteen seniors in both of his first two seasons at CHS. His third season had nine high schoolers who had never played varsity football. Others on the roster were either sophomores, were small in stature or were some combination of the two. His best athletes would always be the ends in the box offense, and some of his best guards in the next three decades may have only been 135 pounds. But when he had "the horses," as he would say, he rode them to success. And his teams had a lot of success.

When he was asked which championship team he was the most proud of, Grisham would reflect on his first team (and his only undefeated team) in 1961, but not for the reason you would think. "We now have four doctors and three pharmacists off that team," Grisham told the *Atlanta Journal* in 1978. "And every one of those players went on to graduate from college—except one." He had sent no more than twenty players to college on scholarships, but Grisham never thought that was the point. It was to make them "better folks for having played the game."

He followed up the '61 title with one three years later at Fitzgerald, where, it was rumored, the county seat of Ben Hill County opened its arms to its competitors—sending word north as soon as possible that every need would be taken care of for the game. A crew 1,500 strong made the trip, enlisting every means necessary for transport—even a previously retired train—to the 20–7 win in one of the muddiest fields anyone can remember. The impression of the Fitzgerald community stuck so strongly with the Carrollton fans that they even sent letters to the editor of the local paper thanking the hosts for their hospitality.

## A REGION RIVAL EMERGES

Coosa High School, just outside of Rome, had to play its first two seasons under Head Coach Branch Bragg in 1956 and 1957 on the road—ten games each time. As the story goes, the school didn't have its own stadium, it just had a pasture. To say it was tough is somewhat of an insult to the word "tough." There were games against rival county schools where Coach Bragg had to fight the mothers of his current players because the last time they had gone to a rival school, the Eagles had left with players with broken legs and had been at the losing end of a 50–0 score. Scheduling Coosa for a homecoming game was the plan for at least six or seven of the schools on their schedule. That would change.

In 1961, Coosa finished the year 12-0 with 8 shutouts, allowing only 21 points the entire season. The team allowed only 6 points through game five, followed by 2 points the following week, 13 to McEachern in a 24-point win and shutouts for their last four opponents—including Lincolnton High 21–0 in the title game played in Athens, where the Eagles were the decided underdog since they had started their program only five years earlier.

In an interview with Randy Davis celebrating the first fifty years of the program in 2005, Bragg said:

> *We were trying to earn respect, since we didn't have any. It didn't come easy. Over the years, our players earned that respect. It wasn't long before it was hard for us to schedule our own homecoming games.*
>
> *That 1961 team was built in 1960. We went 10-0 but lost on penetration by one yard in the playoff their junior year. The people are really what those teams were all about—Ted Goss, Jerry Rucker, Bill Pinson, the Clay brothers and Buddy Gresham…They were fine athletes and good representatives of our program. Doug Trapp was, in my opinion, the finest running back to ever come out of Floyd County.*

Goss had been a guard the year before. Bragg thought that he was the best athlete the team had, so he became the quarterback for the state title team.

Coosa would return for another title in 1969. Enrollment had changed Coosa to its fourth classification of that decade—going from Class C to Class B to Class A, and finally to AA. Bragg's wishbone changed to a wing- T offense that would get through Carrollton, Toccoa and Fitzgerald to get that second title.

"The competition was tougher in 1969," Bragg said. "You had to get through Carrollton. They had won six or seven titles. In the early days before Carrollton, it was West Point High School who had won five or six titles themselves. But we got them, and then we got Carrollton, too."

In 1969, the Georgia High School Association changed the rules on the width of the goal posts and had them widened by three feet. It took a last-minute bit of heroics to make sure the goalposts were regulation for the title game.

> *We had an old booster down here named Glenn Bush. He came down and widened those goalposts for us. The winning points were on a field goal that just got by on the right side by that much.* [Bragg holds out his hands about a foot apart.]
>
> *I definitely remember that one. That team had guys like Gary Graves at quarterback, James Blanton at fullback and a lineman named Bobby Colston. We just about killed him the week of practice before the game with Carrollton because he was doing so badly. But after the game was over, Coach Charlie Grisham came over and shook his hand. That tells you something about the job he did that night.*

Bragg retired as head coach at Coosa in 1974 with those two titles, 140 career wins and only two losing seasons—1962 and 1967. The Eagles have only made it to the quarterfinal round of the playoffs one year since Bragg retired, in 2004.

## SPEAKING OF LINCOLNTON...

In 1957, Buddy Bufford was asked to return to his alma mater of Lincolnton High School to take over a football program that had won only twelve games from 1951 to 1956. Ten of those wins came in the 1955 and 1956 seasons when the Red Devils went an uninspiring 4-6 and 6-4. Red Devil football had seen three winless football seasons in a four-year stretch prior to that and had also seen three coaches in Eddie Martin, Ralph Chambers and Lewis Surls.

Bufford would turn all of that around in three-plus seasons, culminating in the first of many undefeated seasons to come for Lincolnton, LHS and, later, Lincoln County High. Dade High, from the northwest Georgia mountains, came to town heavily favored for the 1960 Class C title game but lost 33–6 to Bufford's team, which placed three Red Devils on the all-state team—including Class C Lineman of the Year Gene Goldman. It was Lincolnton's first of many state crowns.

But there was something else that drove the team from Lincolnton in 1960. Coach Bufford had been diagnosed with cancer in 1959 and was sick most of the 1960 season. His inspiration and perseverance were a motivation not only to his players but also to the community at large during his tenure.

Bufford died on February 24, 1961, at the age of thirty-three, leaving behind a wife and four children. The senior class of 1961 even went as far as using its senior trip money to purchase the archway designating the grounds for what would be the transformed May Field into Buddy Bufford Field.

Another Lincolnton High alumnus, Thomas Bunch, joined the Bufford staff in 1956. With Coach Bufford fighting cancer, Bunch took on the responsibility of running the weekly practice in the 1960 season and, after Bufford's passing, was named head coach. As then Coosa High head coach Branch Bragg just discussed the '61 team, the '62 and '63 teams went 24-0 for two more Class C titles. The 1963 team allowed only two touchdowns, outscoring its opponents 427–13. The Red Devils only allowed one regular-season touchdown to Warren County in their annual rivalry game and the other in the state championship game to West Point High.

If it's any consolation to Red Devils fans, the non-rival squad was the one that converted the extra point, because if you ask anyone in Lincolnton about the Warren County score, they'll debate you to this day that it actually happened.

# A Catamount Is a Mountain Lion

Dalton coach Alf Anderson's likeness at Dalton's Harmon Field.

In 1967, the Dalton Catamounts won their only state title in school history. Bill Chappell had taken over for Alf Anderson in 1963 and proceeded to go 11-2 in 1964, losing in the state title game to Douglas County, 8-3 in 1965 and 9-2-2 in 1966. Chappell went on to win 317, lose only 74 and tie 6. The Cats were a state runner-up six times during Chappell's run, along with eight semifinals appearances and three quarterfinals games. From 1946 to 2007, only four men coached the team— Anderson, Chappell and two longtime Chappell assistants, Bill McManus and Ronnie McClurg.

Chappell remembers:

*In February of 1964, Coach Anderson decided he wanted to be athletic director only. He had been talking about it for three of four years. He lived on Maalox all that time he was coaching. We were standing in the old gym watching some kids play basketball and he told us, "Don't y'all leave. I'll be right back." He goes up to the principal's office and comes back a little later.*

*He says, "Mr. Bowen wants to see you." I'm wondering what I've done, and I'm told Coach Anderson wants to retire. He wanted to know if I'd be head coach. I told them, "I'll sure try." That's all it took. Thirty-three years later I retired.*

# FROM A TO V, IN A ROUNDABOUT WAY

Jimmy Hightower took over as coach at Americus High in 1960. Before he was through a decade later, he would coach two squads to state championships in the middle of the decade in Class A. The first came in 1962, denying Carrollton back-to-back titles in its third straight finals appearance. The second came in 1965 as his team grabbed eight shutouts to start the season and ten shutouts in thirteen games—giving up 27 points total. The Panthers shut out Commerce 14–0 for the perfect ending to an undefeated season.

Dublin High followed up its 1959 title under Head Coach Minton Williams with one the following year over Carrollton in a game played in Thomaston at Robert E. Lee High. Ronnie Baggett had three scores for the Fighting Irish in the 34–20 win. The 1963 title was theirs on the strength of a "made" extra point at the end of the first half in a 13–12 final over Tucker High of Atlanta. Every other attempted conversion, including the one by Tigers quarterback Ron Christopher to go for the lead in the fourth quarter, failed.

Valdosta put a stranglehold on the Class AAA title in the 1960s, winning six outright titles before the end of the decade. The only other teams to win were Avondale, Glynn Academy and Marietta.

The Baze wrapped up three more titles in a row from 1960 to 1962 and gave Bruce Bennett two rings as starting quarterback. Rick Thomas took over for the graduated Bennett in 1962. Between his running and the efforts of Giles Smith, their first win streak went to 37 games before the 2-7-1 team of 1963. The defense of the '62 team only gave up 33 points for the entire season while registering eight shutouts along the way. The other three titles

The game ball from the 1965 title game, found inside the Wildcats Museum.

came in a four-year span from 1965 to 1968. Defense was the highlight of the '68 title team, as they only gave up 31 points in all thirteen games with nine shutouts. The first six games on the schedule were zeroes for the opposition, and the closest margin of victory was a 19-point win in the season opener with Thomasville. Surprisingly, though, only three players were listed as all-staters: back Larry Howell and two interior linemen, Glenn Williams and Walter Jones.

In 1969, Valdosta picked up another state title—but so did Athens High. Athens High quarterback Andy Johnson took his offense down the length of the field for a game-tying score in the waning minutes for the 26–26 tie. People in Valdosta, it is said, didn't get out of bed for days, and many of them didn't attend church on that Sunday, either. Bazemore was set to get the keys to a new station wagon from the Touchdown Club's David Waller as a thank-you gift.

"For us it was like a loss," he admitted. "He didn't want the station wagon, and I didn't want to give it to him. The Athens people? They were going wild."

## AND THE LETTER "W"

Class AA's Waycross High added to Gainesville High's finals frustrations with a 49–0 at City Park in Gainesville in 1960. Junior Marvin Hurst got the first score of the day for the Bulldogs. He would add to his Ware County legend with an admirable performance in his last game as a senior before he would play in Athens for the other Bulldogs at the University of Georgia. His fifty-yard touchdown run on bad knees spread his team's lead to 20–0 at the half before the 23–7 final win over Rossville at Memorial Stadium for the back to back.

Washington-Wilkes and its head coach, Charlie Davidson, made their mark in Class B in the 1960s with four titles in the decade—1960, 1963, 1966 and 1967. Johnny Gresham was all-everything for the Tigers in 1960, wrapping up the year with 228 points as both tailback and kicker. The team's only loss in '60 was to Lincolnton, and one of the two in '63 was to them as well. The Wills brothers, Charles and Bob, paced the rushing attack for the back-to-back titles. Davidson finished his career with a 239-101-14 record over thirty-three years as coach at Washington-Wilkes and later at the Darlington School in Rome.

One of the better nicknames in Georgia high school football is the Screaming Devils of Warren County. Class C had Lincolnton to worry about early in the decade, and they had the team from Warrenton to worry about in the latter half, as the Screaming Devils wrapped up three titles in a four-year span. Legendary head coach Ray Lamb started his head coaching career there and won the first two of those titles, knocking off Monticello in both 1965 and 1966. They faced the Georgia Industrial Institute in the '68 final. The Green Hornets, under Head Coach Walter Davis, had their most successful season in school history, going 9-2 in the northeast Georgia town of Alto.

## DID YOU KNOW…

The Georgia Industrial Institute was initially a tuberculosis hospital constructed in 1928. It would eventually be referred to as a "reform school for boys" by 1952, and the football team ceased by 1973. The name and mission changed to Lee Arrendale State Prison, and by the mid-2000s, it was exclusively a women's prison, with the young men's population sent to the mid-state.

Arrendale warden Tony Turpin, a Habersham County native who began his twenty-four-year career as a guard at the prison, told the *Atlanta Journal-Constitution*'s Carlos Campos in 2004 when the transition was taking place that there was one threat elders always used in the county toward the kids: "If you do wrong, you'll go to Alto."

But for one year, anyway, the institute made it through a run at a title.

## AND FINALLY, A FIRST FOR INTEGRATION—BY NO MEANS A LAST

The year 1966 was the first for integration in the Georgia High School Association, and as per most new things, it took a while for acceptance. Head Coach Joe O'Malley and his Brown High Rebels found out firsthand how different games would be on Friday nights when they lost to Carver-Atlanta High in week four of the regular season, 20–7. Clarence Fisher's Panthers ended up taking Brown's number 7 ranking in the following week's poll, but this was the warning shot for all other schools when it came to misjudging what integration would do for competition.

The Maroon and Grey, by the way, went into week six undefeated before back-to-back losses brought them back from the weekly rankings. Carver finished its season 8-2 and without a postseason bid but went 11-2 the next season before losing to Dalton High for the Class AA state title. The team has fallen on hard times since Fisher's days as coach, but they went 11-1 under Darren Myles in 2007. It's the Panthers community's hope that Myles can bring the school and the football team back to those postseason successes of the past.

Chapter 4

# THE SEVENTIES

## *A NEW ERA*

## THE BEST TEAM EVER?

After a semifinal loss in 1970 to Richmond Academy, Wright Bazemore picked up his thirteenth state title in 1971 after demolishing Avondale 62–12. The offense was one of the more powerful in the modern era of high school football, averaging a little over 48 points per game.

The '71 Wildcats gave Winnersville its third "national" title, and they have been thought of as the best team that ever took the field on a Friday night in the Georgian history of the sport.

The evidence:

Only one team, Ray Goff's Colquitt County/Moultrie High team, was the only team to be within three touchdowns at the end of the game.

The team actually averaged more than one point per minute (48.4 to 48).

The Wildcats averaged more than two hundred yards rushing *and* passing per game.

They scored 40 or more points seven times, 50 or more points once, 60 or more points twice and 75 points in a game against Albany-Monroe High.

Stan Rome's 1,573 yards receiving was the state record for almost three decades.

The 62 points scored in the final still stands as the most points scored in a championship game—regardless of classification.

The Seventies

And then, it was time to go. "I wasn't here from the beginning," Wright's widow Betty recalls, "but I came in 1949. I would jokingly remind him that he had a greater amount of success after he met me."

Bazemore told David Waller and a select few others that, with his health problems, he was going to retire. He told them a few months before the official announcement, and Waller cried on his drive home. It was like a death in the family. Bazemore still played all of his kids, as was his philosophy—regardless of the margin of the score.

What kind of impact did the Bazemores have?

The Arts Council was having financial problems at one point in time during his run. Two local gentlemen wrote a play called *The Baze*. It sold out two nights and helped the arts community.

Betty continues:

> *It shows you what we meant to the community. We'd make an entrance at the end and it brought the house down. They loved Wright, and he loved them and the town. I've never been quite sure of what to really say was the secret of his success. Because he really wasn't a do-it-yourselfer as to which end of the hammer to hold.*
>
> *But he knew football. He had a peripheral vision that he said he got in the navy in Iceland looking on the horizon for German subs. But he could tell what twenty-two people were doing, not just eleven— and I think that was his secret. He could make his moves and his improvements during a game—not having to wait until Monday to see the film.*

Wright Bazemore was a humble man who enjoyed hunting, fishing and his bird dogs. Regardless of who in his hunting party may have shot the game, Bazemore's dogs went hunting and returned them to him. He was the kind of kid who played HORSE in basketball. He would play until he won, and then he'd take the ball and go home. He had a battle with a friend as to who would have tomatoes on the vines faster. Bazemore tied full-sized tomatoes to his vines and won the bet because of how it was worded.

That's the kind of competitor he was on the sidelines, too. Players would bring their report cards to Bazemore—before they went home and showed them to their parents—since academics were first in his mind. Bazemore won ten titles with all-white teams, and then he won four more after the school was integrated in 1965. His career record was 290-43-6.

On December 14, 1971, longtime Georgia newspaper columnist Harley Bowers for the *Macon Telegraph* profiled him, claiming it was "a sad day for the state of Georgia."

"He was The King. There have been none anywhere near his equal and probably never will be. You can rate high school football coaches over any period of time you want, in any way you want and Bazemore comes out several rungs above whoever might be regarded as second best."

Bowers continued:

> *What a joke. No school has a monopoly on material. Bazemore simply knew better how to use it. He made football a way of life for youngsters of Valdosta and they and the entire city benefitted. During his career Bazemore never used a coach in the press box to call down plays. He always refused to swap game film with anyone. He didn't need to.*

He collected win streaks of forty games (1951–54), thirty-seven games (1960–63) and thirty games (1956–58), and by the time of his retirement at the age of fifty-four, his Cats had been unbeaten in thirty-seven of his last thirty-eight games.

"It's kind of sad," Bazemore admitted to Joe Litsch of the *Atlanta Journal* after he retired. "I get these calls from people whose kids are just being born and they want me to hang around so they can play for me."

Head Coach Oliver Hunnicutt of LaGrange put Bazemore's career accomplishments into terms anyone could understand. "If you don't believe Baze was the best high school football coach in the nation," he admitted in an interview with the *Valdosta Daily Times*'s Mike Chason, "look at it this way, if he'd coached ten more years and lost every game, still nobody would beat his record."

"He was the smartest coach that ever lived," David Waller admits. "No doubt about it. I honestly believe that he was."

Bazemore's successor, Charlie Greene, lasted only two seasons despite a 17-3 record. Two years of not getting into the playoffs will do that, as well as not wanting Bazemore on the sidelines in any capacity since he was athletics director.

And where Betty Bazemore would refer to her husband as a "silent Christian," Greene's successor had a verse for his charges every week. Nick Hyder was the preacher. Four times a year when the pastor at the First Baptist Church would leave Valdosta, Hyder would take over the sermons. The Elizabethton, Tennessee native came from West Rome High School, where he had been named Northwest Georgia Coach of the Year for the four years prior to accepting the Wildcats job on February 9, 1974. He felt that he would be coaching "the finest football team playing in the best football town in America"—even when his first year was a 3-7 season. That team would only score more than twenty points twice while giving up thirty or more four times and forty or more twice, with freshman Buck Belue as its starting quarterback. "We both had For Sale signs in our front yards on Saturday mornings," Belue told the *New York Times*'s Drew Jubera in 2007.

Four years later, Hyder won the first of his seven state crowns. He followed Bazemore's grind-it-out, pro-style system to all those titles. "Coach Hyder saved many a kid's life when he coached," Waller continues. "The situation was different than with Coach Bazemore. A lot of the kids that played didn't have a momma or a daddy—or both." Hyder would get up every morning at 4:30 a.m., read the Bible for an hour, leave his wife, June, a note telling her that he loved her and head off to work. He would go straight to the bedroom at 8:00 or 9:00 p.m. after returning from school, watching film from his bed with his dinner on a tray.

Nick Hyder followed Wright Bazemore but set his own path in Valdosta. *Courtesy Wildcats Museum.*

But it is said that Hyder may have made his mark three years earlier at West Rome when, as the top-ranked team in AA, he knocked off the top-ranked team in Class A, the Charlie Grisham–coached Carrollton team. Both were 9-0 going into the last game of the regular season, but the Chieftains won 14–7. That game may have set Hyder up for that trip down south, even if he was upset in the semifinals that season.

# A CHANGE IN LINCOLNTON

There was the 3-7 season in 1972 where Thomas Bunch was an assistant for a team he had coached to a 2-7-1 record the year before. Larry Campbell would admit that Bunch was one of the best assistants he ever had. "That speaks volumes to me, as to what kind of person he was," the new coach told the *Augusta Chronicle* newspaper long after the relationship ended on the field.

Campbell's wife, Connie, made the playbooks for the coaching staff and ham sandwiches for the team on game days, and she washed the uniforms after the games at the local laundromat.

The talk then was that Campbell's tenure might be a short one.

Ham sandwiches or not…

Clean clothes or not…

Things change, and wins change them. And a lot of wins change them a lot.

Larry and Connie Campbell started dating their senior year at Calhoun Falls High School, which had a graduating class of nineteen. There was a college about thirty minutes away that had a small athletic program— Erskine College. They didn't have football, just basketball at the time.

"And I remember stopping her at the water fountain one day and asking if she wanted to go to an Erskine basketball game and it just went from there. When I went off to college we went our own ways and we didn't see each other for a while," Campbell remembers. He went to Anderson Junior College on a baseball scholarship, and she went to Columbia Commercial. She became an airline stewardess based in Atlanta and Miami for Delta Airlines. That "a while" that Larry Campbell refers to turned into about three years.

"Lo and behold, one day," and he starts to smile all over again, "I pulled up to a stoplight. Here I am and here she is and I just asked her if she wanted to go see mom and dad. She got to know them earlier and that was the end

Larry Campbell, the baseball coach who became a legend in football. *Courtesy Mercer Harris,* Lincoln Journal.

of it." They were married in March 1971. Connie commuted back and forth to Atlanta for work, but that ended in July.

When they had been engaged the previous fall, Larry had taken her through Lincolnton for a tour: "You see how small it is here now. Just imagine what it was like thirty years ago. There were just a few buildings. I was here to get the name of the head coach of the baseball program since they were just starting the program up. We came through and I showed her around. She said, 'I can live anywhere for a year.'"

"We were young, newly married and it was exciting," Connie remembers. "We had our son, Brian, at the time. But you don't realize the ramifications of things. I remember Larry coming home and telling me, 'I'm going to be head coach next year.' And I thought, 'Okay.' But you don't really realize how your life is going to go after that."

The Campbells and Connie's parents had taken a trip to Disney World. They were flying back, and Larry found a Delta Airlines postcard in the seat pocket in front of him. He wrote to Thomas Bunch on the postcard that he would accept the job as head baseball coach and mailed it to him—a job accepted by a 3x5.

And that was only the beginning of a relationship that continues to this day.

## SPEAKING OF CARROLLTON...

The run in the 1970s for Charlie Grisham and his Trojans actually started on Trojan Field's turf for a change in 1971. Darnell Turner ran for all four touchdowns as Carrollton beat Turner County 31–21. The Rebels would have to wait five years for a title of their own under Joe Wilson. In 1972, the Trojans took out Mitchell County for win thirteen in fifteen games, taking out the Eagles 34–15 in Camilla. The game had special significance for Grisham, as he defeated his old college classmate Al Woodham.

"Carrollton is a powerful team. And Charlie is a far better coach than he was a football player," Woodham told the local paper, "and you can quote me on that." Tee Reeve, Tony Kight and Jackie Crowder solidified their places in Trojan history, along with names like Chuck Lambert, Trey Traylor, Bryant Wilson, Eddie Jones, Don Proctor, Al Dix and Billy Howard, for back-to-back titles and the fourth for the Grisham era.

The "Three in '73" campaign fell short in a loss to Commerce and "Runt" Moon in the semifinals as Grisham admitted to the Atlanta paper that he had lost everyone on his roster, "including the farmer's duck."

But in 1974, Coach Grisham predicted that it would be his team and the North Springs Spartans playing for the title game as far back as August. Turned out, he was right—but something special happened along the way. The Trojan Booster Club had met in the offseason and decided to name the Trojan Field after Grisham during the '74 season. But on the night of the Central-Carrollton game, the coach almost didn't make it to the ceremony. The team physician, Dr. E.C. Bass, was supposed to get Grisham to stay on the field, but he had to tell the coach that they were honoring someone else—Coach Jimmy Bonner. When Grisham stayed, he found out that his family, ex-players and everyone who could return home were thanking him for his time and efforts on the field at what would become Grisham Stadium at Trojan Field.

"In my wildest dreams I never thought anything like this would happen," Grisham said as it appeared in Bill Fordham's piece in the September 19, 1974 *Carroll County Georgian*, "and it is the greatest honor ever bestowed upon me."

The '74 season ended up with another chance at that third title in four years, as Grisham's team was going up against a North Springs Spartans squad that had held eight opponents scoreless and had the top-ranked defense in Class A. Bob Mangan's teams had registered twenty-five shutouts of their own in the last three seasons and would play with that side of the ball as their trademark. But Sid Sprewell and Bobby Favors led a balanced running attack that had to do something uncharacteristic for a Trojans team—play from behind, as they were down 7–0 early before winning 28–21. And they came from behind with a new wrinkle.

A whopping 18 pounds at birth, five-foot, eleven-inch, 315-pound defensive lineman Billy Howard was brought in as part of a wedge formation that Grisham started using during the playoffs. The "unbalanced line" worked every time it was used in short-yardage situations. Howard won his third title and let everyone else celebrate.

"This is the third time for me," Howard told the *Atlanta Journal*'s Gary Caruso after the game. "I've gotten used to it." As had everyone in Carrollton, no doubt—it was Grisham's fifth in eight tries.

But by the late 1970s, were there chinks in the Carrollton armor? The *Atlanta Journal*'s Lewis Grizzard profiled Grisham, knowing going in that no one knew the last time that the Trojans had started their year losing the first three games of the season as they headed toward a 6-5 year. Grisham's love for his players was still just as strong then as it had been in 1958. If Valdosta's Wright Bazemore was the Vince Lombardi of Georgia high school football in Grizzard's mind, then Grisham was George Halas.

Grisham talks about the pride he feels when a former player is named to the school board. He talks about the hurt he feels when a former player turns out a loser. "Even when I hear of one who hasn't amounted to anything," he says, "I keep thinking maybe he can fall back on the discipline he learned in football. He did it once. He could do it again."

About the losing streak:

> *Charlie said nobody has said anything to his face, He said he hasn't received any hate mail, either. "Not yet, anyway."*
>
> *I doubt that he will...and it's like the guy at the service station was telling me.*
>
> *"Charlie Grisham? Yeah, I know him. He's the finest man in Carroll County."*

Sadly, that would be the end of the titles in Carroll County, as the team wouldn't get past the quarterfinal round for the rest of Grisham's tenure. He retired after a 2-7-1 season in 1986 and gave way to Ben Scott—who had some trophies of his own before his death in 2000.

## BROOKLET'S BACK TO BACK

Southeast Bulloch's two titles in 1972 and '73 for Class B were known more for their offensive prowess than anything. Head Coach Fred Shaver's Yellow Jackets registered nine shutouts in their first 12-0 season, but quarterback David Miller ran an offense that scored more than 50 points twice, more than 60 points twice and more than 70 points four times—maxing out at 76 points in their last regular-season game of the year against Emanuel County Institute (ECI).

They would be the only undefeated team in both seasons for Class B, as they knocked off Duluth 22–8 for the second title. Shaver retired after the game to take a job in administration in Bulloch County's school system. He started the Jackets program in 1966—going 0-10—but finished his coaching career winning 36 of his last 37. The only team that kept him from a three-peat was Bowdon, which beat the team by one point in the 1971 Class B title game.

## MOUNT DE SALES

Coach Mike Garvin came to Mount de Sales Academy in the fall of 1967. He was a mathematics teacher and actually was the head of the Math Department on campus; the subject still is his first love. But in his twenty-three years as head football coach, he brought the Cavaliers three state titles in a four-year span—1970, 1971 and 1973—to go along with his ten career region titles.

Garvin admits:

> *What I learned from Billy Henderson was you play good defense first and then score if you can. We tried that, anyway.*
>
> *If you look at the history of Mount de Sales, they really didn't have a history of winning seasons 'til I got there. I had five sisters who graduated from there as we lived around the corner since it started as a girls' school in*

*its early days. I was really familiar with the school, and people would tell*
*me, "You'll lose over there. You won't win," when I first took the job. I said,*
*"We'll see." What we were able to do there was really gratifying.*

The first two titles came as wins over Adairsville, while the 1973 team had
one of the more celebrated linebackers in University of Georgia history—
Ben Zambiasi. Garvin says, "The first time I ever saw him I knew he was a
football player. He knew what to do when you got to the quarterback, and
when he was being recruited by Erk Russell up at Georgia, he said to me,
'I've got to have that boy,' even if he ran a 4.8 or a 4.9 40."

Ben was a three-year letterman and two-way player for Garvin by the '73
season, with Johnny Henderson (the son of Billy Henderson) at quarterback.
The elder Henderson had left Willingham High in Macon to take a job
in Athens. Zambiasi's father had been transferred to Rhein-Main Air
Force Base in Germany for his military career, so both offensive stars had
interesting living arrangements for that year. Henderson stayed in Macon
with his mother while his dad worked in Clarke County. Zambiasi lived with
Garvin in his basement and became a part of the Garvin family. He even
visits from his Canadian home once every year or so.

The 1973 title game was against the Commerce Tigers and their star
running back, Runt Moon. Moon was the state record holder in yards in a
season with 2,501, and he broke Hawkinsville's Melvin Borum's record for
career touchdowns with 72 for 454 total points. But the Cavs and Zambiasi
ran a six-man front with Zambiasi at middle linebacker to "hold" Moon
to 126 yards in the championship game for the 21–8 win in Tigertown,
breaking the Tigers' thirteen-game win streak. Henderson and Zambiasi
went to Georgia for their college years, and Zambiasi enjoyed a successful
career in the Canadian Football League, eventually ending with an induction
into that league's Hall of Fame.

"1973 was our best team. It was a dream," Garvin says. "The seniors
from the '73 and '74 teams started for us as freshman and sophomores, and
they were good for us as freshmen and sophomores. The experience they
had paid off for us without question. We had played in a Spring Jamboree
in '73 before the season and competed against teams in higher classes. I
knew, then, we'd be really good. I knew we could do it. It was just a matter
of doing it."

The Cavaliers eventually moved from the GHSA to the Georgia
Independent School Association (GISA) to continue their winning ways
across their entire athletic program. But the story would end differently

for Ronald Moon; he is spending the rest of his life in jail due to the sale of cocaine and methamphetamines. In 2006, he was convicted four times for violating the state drug laws before attempting to sell cocaine to an undercover DEA agent in 2005. He was sentenced to life in prison without possibility of parole.

United States attorney David E. Nahmias said at the sentencing:

> *The case of Ronald Perry Moon is especially tragic. Mr. Moon was a star running back on Commerce High School's football team during the 1970s and held the Georgia high school rushing record which was later broken by Herschel Walker. Mr. Moon was a scholarship athlete who played football at Memphis State University and the University of Louisville, but left college in 1978.*
>
> *Between 1983 and 1996, Mr. Moon was convicted four times for violating the drug laws of the State of Georgia. His prior record resulted in a greatly enhanced sentence in this case.*

# BILLY HENDERSON

When Billy Henderson was thirteen years old, he knew exactly what he wanted to do with his life—play professional baseball and be a coach. At the age of seventeen, he played in an all-star game at the Polo Grounds, where he was coached by Ty Cobb. When he made it to the University of Georgia in 1946, he played both football and baseball. On the gridiron, the '46 team beat North Carolina in the Sugar Bowl. The 1947 team played in the Gator Bowl. The '48 team played in the Orange Bowl. And the 1949 team played in the Presidential Cup. Henderson went on to a baseball career, but it didn't last.

"I was so impatient at twenty-two years old," Henderson said in an interview with Georgia Public Broadcasting. "I don't regret it. I didn't stick it out like I wanted to. I was in Greenville, South Carolina, and had just finished a double-header. It was a Sunday. I had a son that was three years old and a wife back in Macon, so I said, 'Well, I'm going to coach.'"

He started his high school coaching career in 1950 in Jefferson, Georgia, but returned home to Macon after eight years to be the head coach at Willingham High from 1958 to 1969. After an 0-7-3 start, he had seven straight winning years before his last four years of .500 football. By 1973, he had taken over Clarke Central High School in Athens—part of the merger of Athens High and Burney-Harris High into his Gladiators in 1970.

Gradual success led to one of his most memorable moments on his way to a title in 1977. It happened the week of Thanksgiving before the quarterfinal win over Newnan. Henderson remembers:

> *We were in the weight room. We had mothers and daddies, girlfriends and families in for devotional prior to going on the field for practice. Mike Walston, our chaplain, was leading our team in prayer, and everybody held hands. And you could just see the tenseness of everybody grabbing everybody tight. Black hands, white hands, rich hands, poor hands, all sorts of hands of every background...*
>
> *I didn't close my eyes. I looked and I thought, "My gosh, I wish everybody in the world had a common denominator like that so we could all have purpose and work together." And it would be a beautiful world.*

The man who was taught by Wright Bazemore not to worry about using the platoon system and to use twenty-two players would grab the 1977 crown by going 14-0 and would repeat the task two years later with 15 wins before the 1980s would add more successes—runner-up finishes in 1984 and 1986, losing both games to Valdosta in the championship with an undefeated season in 1985 sandwiched in between.

## THOMASVILLE GETS A NATIONAL TITLE

Jim Hughes's first head coaching job in the state of Georgia was at Thomasville High in 1970, taking over for Lee Forehand after he had back-to-back 10-2 seasons. Before Hughes left for Colquitt County in 1983, he had the Bulldogs in the national record books for a back-to-back run of their own in 1973 and 1974 while winning twenty-eight of twenty-nine in one stretch in AAA.

A lot of the team's attention centered on the last two seasons of running back William Andrews on the offense. But the defense had fans and media alike paying attention to their efforts. Nine shutouts in 1973 led to a national ranking of thirteenth. Southwest High in Atlanta was actually second in the nation behind Baylor of Chattanooga.

But the 40–35 win in the title game against Wheeler High of suburban Atlanta was disappointing to Coach Hughes, as told to the *Atlanta Journal and Constitution*'s Randy Donaldson: "Our players were cursed, abused, and

The 1974 national champ Thomasville Bulldogs. *Courtesy TvilleBulldogs.com.*

spat upon by the dirtiest team we've played. That's why there wasn't any celebrating. Our kids were disturbed by the nature of the game."

The Bulldogs exacted a measure of satisfaction in '74. Andrews was responsible for three scores in the 26–20 win over Lakeside-Atlanta and was named Back of the Year. The wins down the stretch were good enough for the mythical national title for South Hansell Street.

1974 Final National Sports News Service Rankings

1) Thomasville (12-1)
2) Glenbrook, Northbrook, Illinois (12-0)
3) Harding, Warren, Ohio (11-1)
4) South Hills, Covina, California (13-1)
5) Houston-Brazoswoods (13-1)
6) John Marshall, Rochester, Minnesota (12-0)
7) Morristown, New Jersey (10-0)
8) Gateway, Monroeville, Pennsylvania (11-0-1)
9) Tallahassee-Leon, Florida (13-0)
10) Syosset, New York (9-0)
11) Leominster, Massachusetts (11-0)
12) St. Xavier, Middletown, Connecticut (12-1)
13) Indianapolis-Washington, Indiana (12-0)
14) Holy Name Catholic, Huntington, New York (8-0)
15) Upper Sinclair, Pennsylvania (10-0-1)
16) Putnam City, Oklahoma (11-1)

17) Lakeside-Atlanta, Georgia (11-3)
18) East St. Louis, Illinois (11-1)
19) Upper Arlington, Ohio (11-1)
20) St. John Bosco, Bellflower, California (12-2)

# National Titles Head to Warner Robins, Too

Robert Davis was named head coach in the "International City" in 1973. In only four seasons, he would have his first state title and national title before grabbing both again in 1981 and another state title in 1988. In twenty-four seasons with the Demons, he won all of those titles, along with eighteen region championships. In his thirty-six seasons at Warner Robins and, later, Westside-Macon, he went 353-73-1.

"I think the thing that stands out now is I didn't realize how good we were back then," Davis told Daniel Shirley of the *Macon Telegraph*. "We talk about that now, just how good we were. We didn't really know back then just how good those teams were."

The offensive numbers from the Demons are staggering: never scored fewer than 28 points in a game; four games over 30 points (including the 34–0 championship win over Griffin); four games over 40 points; two over fifty; a 63–0 shutout of Carver-Columbus; and a 90–0 win over Jordan—and for the record, the Red Jackets have only had two winning seasons since 1975. It has taken Jordan High since 1948 to win 188 games total. Davis did that by 1990 at Warner Robins.

James Brooks set the Warner Robins rushing record by the time he left with 4,750 yards and 70 touchdowns—averaging almost 9 yards per carry. Jimmy Womack was Brooks's complement, with Jesse Canion setting a kickoffs-returned for touchdowns record in the process by the time they all graduated. Quarterback Keith Soles still has the highest quarterback passer rating in Demons history—an unheard of 185.06.

From Shirley's article:

> *"Watching Robert Davis do his thing every day, I learned how a football program is supposed to be run," said David Bruce, Veterans' head coach and a former assistant for Davis.*
>
> *Perry head coach Stacey Harden, another former Davis assistant, agreed.*
>
> *"Coach Davis was more than a head football coach," he said. "He knew how to bring out the best in people. He's been a big inspiration."*

In his career, Davis had twenty-one ten-win seasons, and he never had a losing season in all thirty-six years on the sidelines. He had a thirty-year unbeaten streak against the county's schools overall and was inducted into the Georgia Sports Hall of Fame in 2011.

## ANOTHER ROUND FOR AMERICUS

The year after Nick Hyder left West Rome for Valdosta, the Chieftains made their way to yet another title game—this time against Head Coach Alton Shell and the 1974 version of the Americus Panthers. Shell came from his home state of Alabama for the 1971 season and coached at Americus until 1990, when Dan Ragle took over.

Losing to the nationally ranked Southwest Atlanta squad in the 1973 Class AA title game only spurred the team to further success. John Jordan's one-yard touchdown run midway through the fourth quarter gave the team its first championship of the 1970s in a 6–3 win over West. But defense was the way for the '74 squad, as they gave up only 8 points—for the entire season. All-state linebacker Michael Harris led a team that did not surrender any points to a Georgia-based school all season long. Dothan High of Alabama was able to score those 8 points in a week three loss, 14–8. That also served as the closest game the team played all year long. Ray Johnson was fortunate enough to run behind Matt Braswell for a team whose average margin of victory was practically 28–0.

Shell's team finished its unbeaten run at thirty-three weeks in the middle of the 1975 season.

## OH, YOU HERSCHEL WALKER

The town of Wrightsville registered a population of a little more than 2,200 in the 2000 census, with one-third of the families in Johnson County living below the poverty line. But in the late 1970s, one running back from that county drew the attention of practically all the colleges in the United States.

Herschel Walker's junior year for the Johnson County Trojans under first-year head coach Gary Phillips was more of a success than his sophomore season—going from 6-4 and not making the playoffs under Ricky Smith to 9-4 and making it to the quarterfinal round before losing to Charlton County.

The Georgia National Wrestling Alliance's Brandon Brigman caught up with Phillips and asked what everyone thought heading into Walker's senior year:

*We had a good football team the year before and got beat in the semifinals with some kids hurt and banged up, we didn't play very well, but we had a lot of kids coming back. We talked the whole spring practice, the whole summer, we can't let that happen again. We have talent on this team, but we can't get ahead of ourselves either...As a coach that's your goal, win a state championship. I was a track coach, so we wrapped two state championships in track around the one in football. That really made things great. We had great kids and we played under a huge spotlight and our kids responded. That's what I thought was our strength of our team. Our coaches challenged the kids, not only the big names on the team, but the other guys. I firmly believe had we not done that job in the background we would not have won.*

Walker drew a lot of attention after his junior year, but that senior season had college coaches staying in hotels twenty miles away in nearby Dublin. The story goes that Herschel had so many coaches trying to contact him that he couldn't even go to the local 7-11 convenience store without getting bumped into by someone with a college logo on his body.

Phillips told Brigman:

*I remember them saying that they staked out in Dublin and played cards and went to the movies during the middle of the day since there was nothing really to do while Herschel was in school. Herschel had already used up all his visits. Of course, he played basketball so they'd show up at some of his games at night. We got to know most of these guys so we'd take them hunting and stuff to pass the time away.*

The schedule for the Trojans in the 1979 season was a bit different. The region that Johnson County was in was so small that there were multiple games played against three other teams, and all six games were played in a seven-game span. The playoffs even featured a third game against region foe Emanuel County Institute and a rematch against the Charlton County squad that had knocked off the banged-up JCHS team that lost the year before.

Number 43—as he was found in the programs that year—finished up with 3,167 yards and 42 touchdowns. His career total of 6,137 yards would stay for only four seasons, as both ECI's Eddie Dixon and Metter High's Greg Williams fought it out for the top spot by the end of the 1983 season. Dixon won out, 7,322 to 6,920. But for thirty-nine kids who were part of the team along with Walker, they achieved the goal of Class A state champ, and Herschel achieved a few more before he was through as a runner, receiver and kick returner in the United States Football League and the National Football League. Phillips moved on to Riverwood High School in suburban Atlanta for three seasons before he began a career in administration. He is now an assistant executive director for the Georgia High School Association.

"I kept telling everybody we give the ball to the big guy, we're going to be okay," Phillips admitted.

Safe to say they were.

Chapter 5

# THE EIGHTIES

## A NATIONAL PRESENCE

Before the '80s came to a close, the entire country would remember why Valdosta had been a two-time national champ. There hadn't been one of those mythical titles given to the Wildcats since 1971, but that would change. In the decade, Nick Hyder's teams only lost a total of ten games—winning seven region titles, four south Georgia titles, four state titles and two more national ones on their way to a 125-10-1 record.

Valdosta and Clarke Central had three matchups in the finals. The Wildcats won all three of them: 21–14 in 1984, 28–0 in 1986 and 33–13 in 1989. Clarke Central took the crown in 1985 with a win over Warner Robins when Valdosta went an uncharacteristic 9-3.

A balanced running game led the way in 1982 for state title number one. In 1984, Berke Holtzclaw quarterbacked two 1,000-yard rushers in Tony Anderson and Willie Lewis. Future University of Georgia quarterback Greg Talley followed in alum Buck Belue's cleats in 1986 with an efficient passing game and 1,500-yard rusher Jerome Callaway on the way to their crown. And in 1989, Carlos Parker's twenty-four touchdowns was the bell cow for an offense that averaged 25 points per game.

But the Valdosta Wildcats were, more than anything, known for their lockdown defense. Head Coach Nick Hyder's teams registered forty-two shutouts in the decade of the '80s and averaged giving up only a little more than 7 points per game while scoring a little more than 28 per game.

The only team that kept Valdosta out of the mix in 1983 was Tift County. In the last game of the regular season, the fourth-ranked Wildcats "upset"

The 1986 Valdosta Wildcats inside the Wildcats museum.

the second-ranked Blue Devils 14–10 for consecutive win twenty-five. But Tift won the rematch in the region playoff before beating LaGrange in the Class AAAA final, 59–6.

Before Hyder went to Valdosta, he had been the six-year head coach at West Rome High School. Robert Green and Max Dowis set the table after Hyder for Mike Hodges and the start of a historic run of their own in the middle of the decade—four straight championships and an unheard-of win-loss record for those four seasons at 59-1, with three different head coaches at West Rome.

Offensive line coach Tim Nichols admits:

> *We were very fortunate. At West Rome in 1982, we had the Player of the Year in David McCluskey. But he entered high school a quarter behind. The school system moved him up, but it ended up hurting him. It was senior year, but because of the eight-semester rule, he lost his eligibility at the end of November. That was the end of the first quarter. So after the region playoffs, after the region title and after the Feldwood game,*

West Rome High set state football history with its four straight titles. *Courtesy Tim Nichols via* Rome News-Tribune.

*David wasn't eligible anymore. His folks knew it. He didn't. Coach had to wait to tell him. But David was a huge support for the rest of the time before he went on to play halfback and a little tailback at the University of Georgia.*

But it wasn't just McCluskey that got the Chieftains that first title. The names of Floyd, Ivory, Kent, Weaver, Wofford, Hammond, Williams and Green always knew that the idea of "team" was the only way this whole four-year trek was going to get done.

Nichols continues:

*There was no way that we could do what we did without all of us. "We and us is a must" is what we would always say, along with "Team is much bigger than I."*

*But a lot of people don't think that the two years prior to that, we were 8-1-1 and 9-1 under Coach Hodges. Just think if those two seasons had gone the way we'd like for them to have gone, since we beat ourselves, add that to the 15-0, 15-0, 15-0 and 14-1.*

The title game had to be played without their starting quarterback, and Tim Williams had to take over. Mary Persons scored first but missed the point after. West Rome tied the score at 6, but they got their PAT. Everyone will tell you that the kick was one made with authority into the night, but anyone who tells you that story is wrong.

"That thing was a knuckleball that barely cleared the crossbar," Nichols says. "Everyone goes, 'Man, he kicked the daylights out of that thing,' but no. It wasn't like that."

## 1982 (15-0)
## Head Coach: Mike Hodges

| September 3 | Coosa | Win 41–7 |
| September 10 | Dalton | Win 35–6 |
| September 18 | Pepperell | Win 65–0 |
| September 24 | Rockmart | Win 29–7 |
| October 1 | Central (Carrollton) | Win 66–14 |
| October 8 | Darlington | Win 34–7 |
| October 15 | Model | Win 42–24 |
| October 22 | Northwest Georgia | Win 62–7 |
| October 29 | Chattanooga Valley | Win 35–3 |
| November 5 | East Rome | Win 28–0 |
| November 12 | Villa Rica | Win 35–7 |
| November 19 | Cartersville | Win 35–12 |
| November 26 | Feldwood | Win 42–14 |
| December 3 | East Hall | Win 34–0 |
| December 11 | Mary Persons | Win 7–6 |

## 1983 (15-0)
## Head Coach: Mike Hodges

| September 2 | Coosa | Win 12–0 |
| September 9 | Dalton | Win 28–13 |
| September 16 | Pepperell | Win 42–0 |
| September 23 | Rockmart | Win 28–7 |
| September 30 | Central (Carrollton) | Win 42–6 |
| October 8 | Darlington | Win 18–6 |
| October 15 | Model | Win 40–0 |
| October 21 | Northwest Georgia | Win 45–0 |
| October 28 | Chattanooga Valley | Win 45–13 |

| November 4 | East Rome | Win 29–8 |
| November 11 | Cartersville | Win 42–0 |
| November 18 | Central (Carrollton) | Win 14–0 |
| November 25 | Lovett | Win 14–3 |
| December 2 | Duluth | Win 35–11 |
| December 10 | Dooly County | Win 35–0 |

## 1984 (14-1)
### Head Coach: Rodney Walker

| September 7 | Pepperell | Win 36–0 |
| September 14 | Cartersville | Win 21–12 |
| September 21 | Cedartown | Win 21–6 |
| September 28 | Carrollton | Loss 7–0 |
| October 5 | Haralson County | Win 54–7 |
| October 12 | East Rome | Win 34–0 |
| October 19 | Darlington | Win 42–7 |
| October 26 | Model | Win 37–0 |
| November 2 | Coosa | Win 47–0 |
| November 9 | Adairsville | Win 62–6 |
| November 16 | Villa Rica | Win 40–13 |
| November 23 | Central (Carrollton) | Win 20–7 |
| November 30 | Bass | Win 41–0 |
| December 7 | Lakeshore | Win 61–31 |
| December 15 | Mary Persons | Win 14–7 |

## 1985 (15-0)
## Head Coach: Charles Winslette

| | | |
|---|---|---|
| September 6 | Pepperell | Win 35–0 |
| September 13 | Cartersville | Win 41–0 |
| September 20 | Cedartown | Win 49–0 |
| September 27 | Carrollton | Win 41–0 |
| October 4 | Haralson County | Win 48–0 |
| October 11 | East Rome | Win 55–0 |
| October 18 | Darlington | Win 48–0 |
| October 24 | Model | Win 35–0 |
| November 1 | Coosa | Win 21–0 |
| November 8 | Adairsville | Win 28–0 |
| November 15 | Cartersville | Win 31–0 |
| November 22 | Central (Carrollton) | Win 24–19 |
| November 30 | East Atlanta | Win 21–12 |
| December 6 | Lakeshore | Win 28–13 |
| December 14 | Washington-Wilkes | Win 28–10 |

In 1983, West Rome was scared of Dooly County's speed but shut them out. In 1984, the Chieftains got another shot at Mary Persons in Forsyth. But by the time the 1985 season was done, it was more of a relief because of all the expectations that the world seemed to put on this squad. As the story goes, it seemed the entire team got sick after the season came to a close because of all the adrenaline running through West Rome High School after the win over Washington-Wilkes.

But three different head coaches? Even coaches at other schools referred to the revolving door as "bus drivers," since all they needed to do was drop the West Rome players off after picking them up on game day.

Nichols continues:

> *Everybody's different. Every coach was different. The personality of an*
> *adult is geared its own way. But you know who's the most resilient in all*

The headline says it all.
*Courtesy Tim Nichols via*
Rome News-Tribune.

*that? The students, the players…the boys handled it better than anybody.*
*They were concerned about paying attention to the coach. They listened*
*to what the coach said. Thankfully, there were enough of us around to*
*help hold things together. I guess you could say that, as one of the common*
*threads to be there the whole time, you could tell them, "Now, look. This*
*is what the guy wants to do." Those of us who had been there through all*
*of this got to encourage them, and they handled it better than the adults did*
*at the time.*

Each coach had his own philosophies as to how to do things on the
field. The common denominators were hard work, playing good defense,
executing on offense and special teams and believing character will overcome
what you can't put your finger on when things go wrong. The Carrollton loss
is an example of that philosophical approach. The win just wasn't going to
be there on that night, and the question becomes, "What are you going to do
about it?" "Run the table" turned out to be the answer.

Nichols says:

*The players dedicated themselves to be the best. It didn't matter who or what*
*they were playing. They encouraged each other and called on each other to be*
*the best they can be. It wasn't just the coaches, but the teammates as well.*
*That's what makes up a program like that one—excellence. You buy into a*
*program. You buy into the philosophy of doing what's right to be the best.*
*West Rome prided itself on being the best—the way they handled themselves*
*calling on each other and encouraged them spoke to their lives from then on.*

"Their run was amazing," Allen Gossett admits. Gossett was a defensive coach for East Rome High and had the task of trying to stop the Chieftains once a year in a game that was referred to as a "civil war battle."

> *You didn't really believe the run they were on, but you knew it was going to happen anyway. The big thing was you were wondering who was going to score on them in that fourth year. At the time, Region 7-AA had nineteen of the last twenty-three state championships. The teams in that part of the state meant the whole Rome community had to live up to its expectations—West Rome raised the bar for East Rome, Coosa, Model and Pepperell.*

Gossett was a manager on the 1969 Coosa High team, so he had seen it from several angles along the way.

## The Pride of Upson County

Robert E. Lee Institute in Thomaston was regarded as having one of the better teams around in a stretch from 1986 to 1988. The team's last state title appearance had been back in 1961, but behind the running game of Tim Perry and Randy Marshall paired with the quarterbacking of Doug Stanley, the last seasons of the old gold and black made it to a week fifteen game with Washington-Wilkes.

"Our chances are slim and none," Washington-Wilkes coach Marion Brooks admitted to the *Thomaston Times* the week prior. "And that's the truth."

Robert E. Lee High watches as the state title becomes theirs. *Courtesy* Thomaston Times-Enterprise *and the Upson County Archives.*

Actually, Brooks was way off. It took an eighteen-yard field goal from Troy Woodward for the Rebel Hurricane to pull off the 17–16 win. It would also be the last championship for the school, as it dissolved and evolved into the current-day Upson-Lee High School by 1991. The Cadets began play in 1896, playing off and on until 1906 before their first win 40–0 against Boys' High of Atlanta. The program ceased until 1926, and it took a 1957 graduate of the school, Tommy Perdue, to lead the school to a title worthy of a parade, a banquet and a commemorative edition of the *Thomaston Times*. But history in Upson County always will recall that last team.

## LARRY AND LUTHER

Lincoln County High School and Thomson High are separated by a little more than twenty-five miles. The friendship between Larry Campbell and Luther Welsh has seen a lot more miles than that, and the schools that had to face them in the last week of the regular season had to travel a lot of miles themselves to face these two giants of the sport.

Welsh had been a head coach at Warrenton and Dougherty High in Albany before his first tour in Thomson in the '80s. With Jerry Mays and his twenty-eight career touchdowns in 1984 and Terry Pettis as his quarterback, Welsh's first two seasons yielded back-to-back titles by 1985. His Bulldogs were the only undefeated team in AAA, going 29-0-1. It had been ten years since Thomson's last title to go with its two in the 1960s—1967 and 1968.

Larry Campbell ended up winning four of the last five in the decade in Class A. And while defense was the way in 1985, 1986 and 1987 behind players like Douglas, Booker, Glaze and Elam, a freshman got the football in the backfield for the next few seasons—Garrison Hearst. He combined with Stebbin Stokes and Carl Leverett to outrace everyone by 1989. Hearst was given Player of the Year honors for his senior season and was even named an all-stater as a punter. He scored thirty-six touchdowns as a senior, averaging a little over eight yards a carry. He wrapped his career with almost twice as many scores—seventy-one—before heading to Athens and then the National Football League.

But if you ask the folks over at Washington-Wilkes, they may remember knocking off the Red Devils in 1986. The win ended the Tigers' ten-game losing streak in the rivalry, but they finished runner-up in AA, going 14-1.

# THE RUN OF THE BULLDOGS FROM FORSYTH

"You build a program by playing great defense, be solid in the kicking game and don't let your offense beat you early," says Sandy Creek High School head coach Chip Walker on the best advice he got from Dan Pitts.

Dan Pitts already had a job as an assistant under Billy Henderson at Willingham High School (now Southwest-Macon) in Macon. But when he heard that the head coaching job at Mary Persons High School in Forsyth—about thirty minutes north of Macon—was open, he went for an interview. He visited then-principal Jim Mitchell, asked for the job and got it.

On September 4, 1959, he debuted as the Bulldogs' coach in a loss to Monticello, 13–0. Pitts said he had just eighteen players during one of those early years and went 2-8 in that rookie year. Pitts went on to become the second-winningest coach in Georgia high school history with a 346-109-4 record. He led the Mary Persons Bulldogs to five undefeated seasons, sixteen region titles and a state title in 1980. The 1980 team registered eleven shutouts, giving up a total of 48 points (and 28 of those in the rivalry game against Lamar County) on their way to that lone title in Pitts's history—winning 34–6 over Duluth in week fifteen.

"They just wanted it," Pitts told the *Monroe County Recorder* in its thirtieth-anniversary article looking back on the team. "They played really well. We had a little bit more talent in 1979. But they played really well, and the defense was outstanding. We were probably better on offense in 1978 and 1979. And two starters were put off the team right before the season started that got in trouble with us."

But Pitts's style was unmistakable—practice one aspect of the game one day, another aspect of the game another—no mixing. Some of his better offensive players would go both ways if needed, but the defense was stout across the board.

"We had some real good football teams, and we played for [the state title] four times," said Pitts, whose team made the finals in 1980, 1982, 1984 and 1993. "But there are some things that mean more to me than the state championship. That's not the highlight. The highlight is that I was here, and that I enjoyed it very much."

Pitts's early years had more losses than wins. As a matter of fact, three of his first four seasons had losing records, including an 0-10 year in 1961. But the coach admitted that when he started, there were one hundred dairy farms in the county, and he tried to balance the kids' free time and

Dan Pitts Stadium in Forsyth, the home of the Bulldogs.

practice time with their chores at the farms and hay fields. If there was some discontent from the people of Monroe County, he never heard it firsthand, and he was pleased that the kids played as hard as they did in a year that had his Bulldogs shut out four times while giving up double digits every week on defense. By the way, his last losing season was 1965 in a career that went another thirty-two years on the sidelines.

"I retired a year after I wanted to," Pitts admitted in the retrospective in the *Recorder*. "I wanted to retire the year before. I didn't tell anybody, not even my wife. But I thought that last year [1996] wasn't going to be strong and said I won't leave on that. But actually we did all right, and went two deep into the playoffs. I was real happy about how they turned out."

That last loss was to Rick Tomberlin and the Golden Hawks of Washington County.

# Charlie Grisham Retires

After a 2-7-1 season in 1986, the Carrollton icon decided to retire—not because of that last season at Trojan Field or the quadruple-bypass surgery he had the year before after a heart attack in December 1985, but because of a diagnosis of narcolepsy, a disease he inherited from his father.

"It's more aggravating than crippling," Grisham told the *Carroll Times-Georgian*. "It affects the things I should be doing. I can be sitting here at the desk and just nod off. A specialist in Atlanta told me I had as true a case as he's ever seen." In May 1987, Charlie Grisham Appreciation Day was held. Former players from his state title teams spoke on the impact Grisham had on their lives, but two who weren't known for titles gave just as impassioned speeches on Grisham's legacy.

Garvin Boyd was the first black athlete to play for Carrollton High School, and Grisham had a choice—a decision tough for some but not tough at all for Grisham. "He made the decision based on it being the right decision and that decision probably gave me the opportunity to get a football scholarship and continue my education. He taught us that an average person can do extraordinary things if you work hard enough," Boyd said.

Ben Garrett was quoted in the *Times-Georgian* as well from the ceremony. Garrett was a senior who was part of the last Grisham team to take the field on Friday nights and had a perspective no one else could provide: "All of you have not played for a losing football team at Carrollton," Garrett admitted. "I have. It was his first losing season. But I can assure you that he was every bit as gracious losing as he was winning. I would not trade a state championship for what I learned. He is special to the community and to me."

The Booster Club presented Grisham with a portrait that would hang in the soon-to-be completed field house and a check for more than $10,000 that was going to be used to help build a fishing cabin for Grisham.

Sports editor Jim O'Hara summed up the Grisham legacy this way: "Charlie Grisham will be leaving a legacy behind him that few will be able to accomplish. But more noticeable will be the memories he has left in the minds of those who were around him."

Grisham took himself out of the search for a replacement, but it ended in Athens with an assistant coach for Billy Henderson at Clarke Central High School. Ben Scott was the offensive coordinator for a Gladiators squad that went 65-5, including 49-1 in the regular season, and possessed a 29-game win streak. All five years under Scott yielded region titles, two runner-up performances in AAAA in 1984 and 1986 and a state title in 1985. Each year Scott was on campus, Clarke Central was ranked top five in the state and top twenty-five in the country by *USA Today*. He coached four all-state quarterbacks as well. The Trojans were left in good hands with the West Point grad.

# Chapter 6

# THE NINETIES

## *A TIME OF DOMINATION*

## MORE NATIONAL RECOGNITION

Gary Guthrie followed Jimmy Hightower and Danny Cronic as head coach after Hunnicutt's retirement from LaGrange High School in 1971. Guthrie's and Hunnicutt''s approaches were different, but they were equally as successful. Guthrie even won a national championship in 1991.

LaGrange football historian Scott Sickler, LHS class of 1980, says:

> *It was an amazing season in many areas but in the end it was a terrific, speedy and super physical defense which made the '91 Grangers a truly great team. The 2011 season marks the twentieth anniversary and Walt Harris, a defensive back on our championship team, was still playing in the NFL as of the 2009 season—a remarkable achievement unto itself. Rodney Hudson was a superb athlete and made many big plays (who can forget the game-winning drive in the last minute at Colquitt Co.) but make no mistake, it was the "Storm Trooper" defense which was the backbone of the team. Senior Bubba Scott and junior Paul Pickett played both ways the entire season—talk about iron men, they were, especially with the schedule LaGrange faced.*
>
> *LaGrange's legendary 6–0 win over Nick Hyder's vaunted Valdosta Wildcats [then number one in GHSA AAAA and number two in the USA Today poll] put the Grangers in position for greatness.*

*LaGrange was No. 2 in AAAA behind Valdosta—riding a thirty-three-game unbeaten streak—and number eight in the* USA *Today poll. Pre-game hype was off the charts, and rarely does such a game live up to its billing, but this one did and then some. There was more talent on the field at the LaGrange-Valdosta game in 1991 than what you'd find at college games—loaded on both sides. The win over Valdosta put LaGrange at number two in the* USA *Today poll, behind number-one-ranked California Rialto-Eisenhower.*

*A chopper pad was set up at Callaway Auditorium, across the street from Callaway Stadium. I counted eight helicopter landings with media from around the Southeast and some national stringers to cover the game including Atlanta, Macon, Albany, Columbus and Jacksonville. That won't ever happen again.*

*The three-game close to the state and national championship against Valdosta in the quarterfinals, McEachern in the semifinals (20–14 in overtime) and state championship against Colquitt County has to rank as one of the greatest runs in state history, at least in terms of excitement. A lot of people forget it was the home win over rival Newnan and Max Bass which set up LaGrange on its string of home playoff games. The 1991 season at LaGrange was truly a special season and although it's been matched with three more state championship teams* [2001, 2003 and 2004], *including two perfect season squads in 2001 and 2004, the living-on-the-edge Grangers in '91 won't be duplicated.*

By 1991, West Rome High School and East Rome High School were being squeezed in by all the commerce that was popping up in and around both campuses. East Rome was losing enrollment, and the prevailing wisdom was that having one school—the soon-to-be-created Rome High—would be better than the two smaller schools. The Wolves have made it into the playoffs fairly frequently since their 1992 debut and even made it as deep as the semifinals in 2008. But a lot of people on both sides of the East Rome–West Rome side picking feel that the Chieftains and Gladiators think they're being forgotten in all of this history while the traffic and commerce continue to grow.

Tim Nichols says:

*I think you just need to describe the East Rome–West Rome rivalry as "fun." There were a lot of guys who just knew each other and grew up around each other. The way the dividing line was drawn for the two schools,*

East Rome High today—yes, it's a K-Mart.

West Rome High today—yes, it's a Walmart.

> *the kids really did grow up across the street from each other. They went to
> church with each other and loved to compete against each other. It was like a
> neighborhood ball game, and that's what made it fun. It didn't take a whole
> lot of motivation to get them to compete with each other.*

And now it's the adults who get to tell the stories of another town, once
divided, that isn't any longer. They're not the only ones, either.

# THE EMERGENCE OF WASHINGTON COUNTY

Before Rick Tomberlin's tenure in Sandersville, the longest amount of time any coach had been on the sidelines was four years dating back to the school's opening in 1959. Tomberlin stayed for fourteen seasons and caused everyone to know where Washington County is on a Georgia map, with talented players with the names of Spikes, Edwards, Horn, Miller, Wright and many others.

Admittedly, it was hard to get coaches to join Tomberlin's staff in Sandersville since it would qualify as "the middle of nowhere." But in his first year, 1992, his Golden Hawks made it all the way to the state title game before losing to Jack Johnson and Mitchell-Baker—one of two titles the Eagles would bring to Camilla in the '90s. In 1993, WaCo started out as number one in the state, won twelve straight after an opening week loss to Dublin and lost 14–13 to Dan Pitts and Mary Persons. It was the only time that the Bulldogs would get the best of Sandersville.

But by 1994, the question was, could Washington County ever win the "big one"? It wouldn't be a question after December.

The Golden Hawks set the state scoring record with 631 total points, went 15-0, won a state title and thought that their run was the football equivalent of a "moon shot" for Sandersville. The team's output was so powerful that in ten of the fifteen games, Tomberlin didn't play his starters in the third quarter. And there is also the prevailing thought that winning a state title is like winning the Miss America crown. You definitely feel no pain for a while.

One linebacker particularly stood out for Tomberlin's defense in those early years. "That first practice with him," San Francisco 49ers linebacker Takeo Spikes recalls, "everybody was doing a lot of brown-nosing. It was strange, though. You had a new guy coming in to coach and no one had any idea what to expect. But you had a lot of people out there trying to show him, 'Okay, I'm your player. I'm your man at that position.' It was clueless for everybody, but they were trying to do whatever they could to show themselves to him as a player."

"I can still hear Coach Tomberlin to this day," Spikes told Jeff Sentell of the *Augusta Chronicle* years later. "He always used to shout, 'You're either getting better or getting worse today. You never stay the same,' on the practice field. That's never left me through all my levels of football."

"He was the most driven and goal-oriented player I have ever been around," Tomberlin said of Spikes. "Takeo always burned to be a champion. I wasn't surprised when he became an All-Pro in the National Football League."

A hit on Mary Persons running back Quentin Davis in the 30–14 quarterfinal win personifies that desire and WaCo's place in the high school stories of the 1990s. "Spikes meets that young man helmet-to-helmet on that play and just decimates him," Tomberlin said. "It was the single greatest hit I have ever seen in high school football. The stadium was set underneath hills. I tell you that hit sounded like a rifle shot from the tree line from those hills. We dominated that team from that point. One hit totally changed the tone of that football game."

By the time Spikes was done, the Golden Hawks had set a record in that 1994 season for most points scored by any Georgia high school team in history regardless of classification. There was that feeling in the field house that the team was a special lot and could accomplish what they did.

"I went out with a title," Spikes said. "I walked off that field for the last time as a Washington County player knowing that the first chapter of my football life was completed in the best way."

Tomberlin knew that athletes like Spikes and Robert Edwards were special. In those early years, going 41-3, Washington County developed a tradition and an expectation in a town that hadn't experienced consistent success. College coaches would tell the Golden Hawks that they were playing football the way it was supposed to be played. But it was the athletes who may not have been the most talented that made the program what it was. They wanted to play like a Takeo Spikes, a Robert Edwards or a Jesse Miller. They would all play bigger because of the influences around them. All they ever did was "roll up their sleeves and go to work."

The 1995 team was loaded with sophomores and went 7-4, but the following year, all those sophomores were juniors and ran the table again with a 15-0 year. The title came in a come-from-behind 22–21 win at Americus. Down 14–0 at the half, things got worse for the Golden Hawks as Terrence Edwards tipped a pass that was caught for another score.

"After that play, I literally shoved Tyree Williams off the field because he was walking off," Tomberlin admits. "I told him, 'Don't walk off the field.' And after that play, we caught fire. They just couldn't stop us."

The '97 team of seniors went undefeated again and was regarded by a lot of different people as one of, if not the, best team in the state. Tomberlin admits that he was pleased with his 1994 and 1997 teams as they dealt with the pressure of being top-ranked in the state and making it out the other side with a championship. The playoff run included another win in Forsyth against Mary Persons, a semifinal win against Pepperell at the Georgia Dome and the game fifteen win in Carrollton.

Tomberlin admits:

> *It was a very special time for all of us. I'm very proud of what we accomplished. If you go back to the time after the 1997 title all the way through to 2005, we were still playing for state championships in AAA. And I still think we were one of the best programs in the state the entire time.*
>
> *I really believe God had a hand in our success in Sandersville. It was a great fit. We had great players and it was a town of wonderful people. The kids worked hard in the weight room. They worked on their agility and speed. We drove, pushed and challenged them in the summers. There was toughness and there was tough love. It was like playing for the Green Bay Packers or living in Camelot. It was high school football in its purest form.*

And when Tomberlin took a coach's trip to Notre Dame in the spring of 2011, even some of the people on the South Bend campus marveled at the idea of winning more than 150 games in fourteen years. Knute Rockne only won 112 games in his twelve years on campus.

Tomberlin says, "There's not enough money in Fort Knox for all those memories. I can't brag, salute or recognize all of them enough. Years later, you know you were part of a very special run."

## A SHOCK IN VALDOSTA

In 1996, Nick Hyder had a heart attack in the school cafeteria and died. More than eight thousand people viewed his coffin—in the school colors, black and gold—on the stadium's fifty-yard line.

Wright Bazemore, who had a black and gold coffin made for himself, donated it to the Hyder family. Bazemore suffered a debilitating stroke in 1996, but that didn't keep him from keeping an eye on Hyder's successor, Mike O'Brien.

David Waller was the head of the board of education at the time of Hyder's death. Contracts had been signed for the following year, and there was an immediate search that included some past coaches. One, Jack Rudolph, turned down the job—even for a year—because his two best friends were Bazemore, who was fighting the effects of the stroke, and Hyder, who had just died. He wouldn't take the job "for a million dollars."

Bazemore-Hyder Stadium at Cleveland Field, home of the Wildcats.

An assistant since 1981, Offensive Coordinator O'Brien took over in late May of that year and won a state title in 1998. But four years later, he was fired after compiling a 70-20-1 record. At the time, he attributed his dismissal to disagreements with powerful boosters.

"There was a group that wanted more input into who the new coach would be after Coach Hyder died," said O'Brien to *Georgia Trend Magazine*'s Jerry Grillo in a 2004 interview.

"There's a different sense of appreciation here [at Woodstock]. It's a young program, but I'd like us to reach the point where we have the same expectations we had in Valdosta."

Bazemore reportedly had another Wildcat-colored casket made for himself by the time he died in June 1999. Hyder's friend Waller donated a space in his Waller family plot at Sunset Hills Cemetery for the fallen coach. "He was my best friend in the world," says Waller, who played for Bazemore fifty-odd years ago. "That was a tough time for all of us because everybody loved Nick. Even his bitterest rivals at Lowndes County and Colquitt County liked him. And he knew the Bible better than most preachers."

Bazemore and Hyder still have their impacts on their players to this day. One of Wright Bazemore's players, Pat O'Neal, opened a barbeque joint in town. He had a soft launch with some VIPs and wanted Betty Bazemore to show up on that day. O'Neal told her, "I just want to show you what coach taught me—giving 110 percent and when you're down, get back up."

"So, it's still going on," Betty said with a smile in an interview with the *Valdosta Daily Times*, "not just winning, but making a wonderful life in these boys."

## CHAPPELL SAYS GOODBYE

Dalton High's Bill Chappell. The plaque is at the stadium that bears his name.

Bill Chappell, coach of the Dalton Catamounts, had a triple-bypass in March 1994. When Alf Anderson learned that the best rehabilitating that could be done was walking, he would show up at 603 Wilkins Street to get his successor up and moving—from the first day he was able. Spring practice led to fall practice, but Bill Chappell started hearing voices.

"There was this voice," Chappell admitted. His voice lowers, and he still tries to register where the voice actually came from. "It was saying, 'Back off!'

"I went home and talked to my wife. I told Bennieta I was hearing voices. She told me that I wouldn't know what to do with myself. I was best under pressure. I told her that she didn't understand. I'm HEARING VOICES!"

He started backing off in his coaching intensity. The next season, he started hearing the voices all over again. Before the season started, he was a pallbearer for his friend, Gainesville head coach Bobby Gruhn. Chappell's mother died during the playoffs. Coach Anderson died that February. And then there was Hyder. It was too much.

"Bennieta was riding with me to the Hyder funeral, and I had been hearing voices telling me to stop for two years. The next season 1996, was going to be my last.

"I'm not going to drop dead in a cafeteria.

"I'm not going to drop dead on a football field.

"I'm not going to do it.

"She tells me, 'I think you're ready.'

"I told her I was ready two years ago."

In the beginning, Chappell had only intended to stay at Dalton for two years before moving on. He was only off by forty-two years. And Bennieta will always tell Bill she was the best recruiter he ever had—especially when she taught elementary school.

# WHERE'S FOLKSTON?

Rich McWhorter came down from Illinois and was the only coach to apply for the Charlton County head coaching position when he took the job—or, more accurately, when it was given to him as his own funeral. If only every funeral could be like McWhorter's.

Before his first season, the Indians' last winning season had been in 1979, when the team went 7-4 under David Stephenson. McWhorter hasn't had a losing season in his entire tenure there, and he even got to a title game in his first season, 1990.

"We played Lincoln County and lost 6–0," McWhorter remembers. "You think that it may, quite possibly, be my only chance. It may not ever come around again." It wasn't. Charlton appeared in four more quarterfinal matches before grabbing its first title in 1999.

"You look at it now and the later in the year it got, the harder I pushed them. You had to create hardships like brutal practices and things like that. You had to do that to keep them moving forward," McWhorter says.

But Charlton traveled to Lincoln County and got its shutout returned to it for the Class A title, 20–0. "Everyone started jumping the fences," McWhorter continues. "It was a heck of an atmosphere. You wish every kid could experience it just once. I was with the other coaches asking, 'Can you believe it?' I've been a head coach for twenty years and to be able to be with a special frat to be called a 'champion'? You feel different."

And when the Bailey family is part of your successes in the 1990s, it would lead to more success in the next decade as well.

## LINCOLN COUNTY CONTINUES

The Red Devils would have their stamp on Class A again in the 1990s with six finals appearances and three titles to show for Lincolnton's efforts. They started the '90s where the '80s left off—an undefeated season and a title over Charlton County as Anthony Parks and Carl Leverette took over where Garrison Hearst left off. A loss in the title game in '91 alternated with two more undefeated seasons in '93 and '95. The Red Devils appeared in back-to-back title games in 1998 and 1999 but lost both to Darlington and Charlton County. Larry Campbell's titles increased to nine by the end of the twentieth century.

## THE END OF AN ERA

Carrollton's Charlie Grisham passed away in 1999, and he had a simple request: "He said, 'There was three things that I would like: I would like to have a Christian burial, they sing "Amazing Grace" and set up a scholarship in my name,'" noted one of Grisham's three sons, Burt Grisham, in an interview with the *Carrollton Times-Georgian*. "So I think we were able to do all three."

The third wish comes to life every year in the form of a charity golf tournament, the Charlie Grisham Memorial Golf Tournament, which benefits Carrollton High School and the Carrollton City Schools Education Foundation.

"Obviously, we're doing it to raise money for the scholarship. But we hope by doing that it does keep his name out in front of the community and help people remember that he was a great Trojan," another of Coach Grisham's sons, Glynn, said. "We pull out memorabilia from the old days. We've just got a lot of articles about the football teams that a lot of these guys played in. You know, it's a lot of fun."

Grisham never thought of leaving for a college job and grew to love the town that had been good to him for a very long time. Carrollton would think the exact same thing.

# THE RUN OF THE YELLOW JACKETS

Ed Pilcher had a successful five-year run at Early County High School in Blakely before taking over at Thomas County Central in 1991. His first seven years at the Jacket's Nest brought five state titles: 1992, 1993, 1994, 1996 and 1997. Pilcher and his staff rode the veer offense to playoff successes until his departure in 2007 with one exception—a 4-6 season in 2004.

The 1992 team got off to an un-playoff-like start of 1-5. After that last loss, a 19–0 shutout by Westover, Pilcher went to an unconventional lesson at practice. He had his players practice touchdown celebrations.

"We just started playing better football," former Central wide receivers coach Eugene Conner told the *Thomasville Times-Enterprise*'s Clint Thompson. "We had some guys that wouldn't quit on you."

The Jackets then ran the table for nine straight weeks, hardly challenged until the semifinal round of the playoffs. Week fourteen was a 20–14 win over Stephens County, where Central even let Stephens County score late in the fourth quarter so they could get possession of the football again. "We probably wouldn't have won if we hadn't let them score," said Conner.

And then, a 14–13 win over Peach County gave TCC its first state title.

Two more titles in '93 and '94 got the team noticed around the state but also served notice to all the players coming up through the system as to what they were getting themselves into as they got older. "We would watch all the older guys and we didn't want to stop the run," tailback Joe Burns said. "At the middle school level, we went undefeated in our eighth-grade season. We saw the pressure the guys were going through in '92 and '93 and when we were freshmen in '94. We saw how hard they worked, and we didn't want to let big brother down."

The only hiccup in the streak came in 1995 as a second-round loss to Kendrick sent the sophomore stars home early, but 1996 was a comeback year. As a junior, Burns ripped off 2,006 yards and thirty-two touchdowns for their offensive prowess, as well as one of the most-recalled semifinal games in state history. At the Georgia Dome, Thomas County Central was in a back-and-forth battle with Marist that went to overtime. Pilcher knew he couldn't trade blows with the War Eagles.

In overtime, he called a halfback pass-option for Burns, who, by his own admission, was a horrible passer. "I was surprised he called it in the time out," Burns said. "He said, 'We can't stop them. We're not going for the extra point. I trust you. And whatever happens, I appreciate ya'll.' I wasn't nervous. It was going to be the win or loss right there. All we had to do was execute. I got the pitch and saw Alphonso [McKibbens] in the end zone and I hit him a few inches from the back. He was almost out of bounds.

"But that trust Coach had in me and my teammates really got us going. It made all the hard work and sacrifice worth it."

The 22–21 win over Marist was the tougher game of the last two, as they walked over Lakeside-Atlanta 41–9 for their third title in a four-year period.

The '97 squad was probably the most dominant team of that whole run for Pilcher, with the backfield of Burns and quarterback Leonard Guyton. The team would normally score in the thirties. But there were outbursts of forty-five, fifty-three, fifty-five, sixty-nine and seventy-three points on scoreboards along the way. Burns's last high school game was capped with a 237-yard rushing performance in the state title win over Burke County. Quarterback Leonard Guyton had more than 2,000 all-purpose yards on his own in that offense.

"We never really got tested real good," said then Central assistant (and now Thomas County Central head) coach Bill Shaver. "We had a lot of blowouts that year."

Guyton and Burns were all-state performers, as were linebacker Raytorrie Newkirk and defensive back Chris Daniels.

"I really believe that was the best team we had at Central," said Conner, who served as Central's offensive back coach in 1997. Burns received Region 1-AAAA Offensive Player of the Year honors after both his junior and senior seasons. He followed the 2,000-yard junior year with a 1,941-yard and twenty-four-touchdown season as a senior.

"Joe is obviously one of the best players to come out of Central," Central coach Ed Pilcher told the *Times-Enterprise*'s Jamie Wachter at the time. "He wasn't blessed with an overabundance of athleticism, but boy what a heart. He was one of the best players we've had."

Burns went on to a college career at Georgia Tech and followed that up with some time in the National Football League with the Buffalo Bills. Guyton played in college at NCAA Division II powerhouse Carson-Newman.

"We had a special group," Burns told Wachter. "We stuck together. Even in middle school, we went undefeated. We just had a little swagger about us. We had Leonard Guyton. We had Raytorrie Newkirk. We just had great players, great athletes. We just kept that same swagger, going over to the high school."

"The bigger the challenge, the better he [Burns] responded," Pilcher said. "I've never seen a young'un that responded so much under pressure the way he did. The tougher the situation, his level of performance—

whether it was in the classroom or on the field—it just rises, and that's unusual for a high school kid."

A lot of opposing teams thought that when Thomas County Central took the field, it was a joke because they were a bunch of "little guys," according to Burns. But they had run the same offense since middle school, and they proved themselves on Friday nights when the other team on the field stopped talking.

"We never dreamed," Burns says with wonder, "of that kind of accomplishment by the time we were through."

## THE NORTHERN PURPLE HURRICANE

Cartersville's version of a hurricane would book-end the decade with two titles to show for their work, and they would do it on the ground both times. Class AA Player of the Year LaShon Darby would run for almost 1,600 yards on the ground- 213 of them in the title game against Cedar Grove High for title number one and Ronnie Brown would make his name known under Frank Barden's 1999 squad with their win over Hart County for title number two.

Brown would go onto successes in college at Auburn and in the pros, currently with the Miami Dolphins. The six-year vet has one 1,000-yard season under his belt. When healthy, he has proven to be an elite NFL back and is already top five in team history in rushing attempts, rushing yards, and touchdowns.

## DAN PITTS RETIRES

Senate Bill 756 was passed during the 1998 General Assembly, courtesy of Representative Edwin Gochenour from the Twenty-seventh District around Forsyth:

> WHEREAS, in his 39 years of coaching, Dan Pitts and his teams achieved an awesome record of 346 wins, 109 loses, and 4 ties, making Dan Pitts the second winningest high school football coach in all of Georgia's history; and
>
> WHEREAS, during his illustrious career at Mary Persons High School, the football team accomplished five undefeated seasons, sixteen regional championships, and a state championship in 1980; and

*WHEREAS, Dan Pitts has been honored many times for his outstanding accomplishments as a coach, having been voted a four-time coach of the year for all of Middle Georgia by The Macon Telegraph (1980, 1982, 1985, and 1991); the State at Large Coach of the Year by the Georgia Athletic Coaches Association (1980–81); the Class AA Coach of the Year by the Atlanta Touchdown Club (1980 and 1984); and Coach of the Year by the Georgia Athletic Directors Association (1990); and*

*WHEREAS, in 1987, Dan Pitts received the Georgia Athletic Coaches Association's prestigious Dwight Keith Award; and*

*WHEREAS, Dan Pitts has shared these 39 years of hard work and victories with his wife, Mary Lynda Pitts, and their two daughters and three grandchildren.*

*NOW, THEREFORE, BE IT RESOLVED BY THE SENATE that the members of this body commend Dan Pitts for his outstanding record as head coach of the Mary Persons High School football team and for the enduring and positive impact he has had upon the students who have been members of that football team since 1959 and extend our heartiest best wishes upon his retirement.*

Dan Pitts would get to spend more time watching his grandkids play football rather than coach on the sidelines after his retirement. Steve Chafin took the Bulldogs to the semifinals in 1998 before bowing out to Early County. That same year, Rodney Walker got a state title for Peach County in Fort Valley, knocking off Dougherty High. Walker eventually succeeded Chafin after the 2005 season after building the Sandy Creek program for his son, Chip. We'll find out more about Chip's successes in the next chapter.

Chapter 7

# THE TWENTY-FIRST CENTURY

The start of the new century yielded a few interesting elements right off the top. The first was the expansion of football to five classifications instead of the long-standing four, which had been the way of division since the last reorganization in 1972. The second was the emergence of a variety of south Georgia schools in claiming championships come game fifteen of the season. But it was an Atlanta school that got the decade started off with an unequalled streak. And that's what the decade was, in a phrase—a decade of streaks.

After its '97 AAAA title, Parkview was part of the expansion to AAAAA, and it made sure everyone knew who was boss for the next three years. From September 2, 2000, to September 12, 2003, the Panthers put a forty-six-game win streak on the board that a lot of people thought would stay unmatched for a while.

## 2000 Parkview Panthers (15-0)

| September 2 | Harrison | 8–7 |
|---|---|---|
| September 8 | Norcross | 10–3 |
| September 15 | Dacula | 14–7 |
| September 29 | S. Gwinnett | 21–0 |
| October 6 | Berkmar | 26–7 |

| October 13 | Shiloh | 14–10 |
| October 20 | Brookwood | 18–17 |
| October 27 | Duluth | 33–7 |
| November 3 | N. Gwinnett | 27–8 |
| November 10 | Collins Hill | 35–14 |
| November 17 | Redan | 24–0 |
| November 24 | Roswell | 28–7 |
| December 1 | East Coweta | 31–10 |
| December 9 | Westside-Macon | 27–0 |
| December 16 | Harrison | 19–7 |

## 2001 Parkview Panthers (15-0)

| September 7 | Norcross | 21–19 |
| September 21 | Berkmar | 45–0 |
| September 28 | South Gwinnett | 17–14 |
| October 12 | Shiloh | 44–10 |
| October 19 | Brookwood | 24–7 |
| October 26 | Duluth | 42–7 |
| November 2 | North Gwinnett | 27–0 |
| November 9 | Collins Hill | 21–0 |
| November 16 | Dacula | 38–7 |
| November 23 | Douglass | 36–0 |
| November 30 | Roswell | 24–21 |
| December 7 | Westside-Macon | 35–6 |
| December 14 | Valdosta | 30–14 |
| December 22 | Northside–Warner Robins | 12–7 |

## 2002 Parkview Panthers (15-0)

| August 31 | East Coweta | 21–0 |
|---|---|---|
| September 13 | Brookwood | 17–10 |
| September 20 | Berkmar | 44–0 |
| September 27 | Collins Hill | 31–0 |
| October 4 | Central Gwinnett | 28–0 |
| October 11 | Meadowcreek | 58–0 |
| October 18 | Norcross | 43–7 |
| October 25 | Oconee County | 46–0 |
| November 1 | Shiloh | 48–7 |
| November 15 | Duluth | 58–6 |
| November 22 | North Cobb | 34–15 |
| November 29 | Centennial | 49–0 |
| December 6 | Northside–Warner Robins | 21–19 |
| December 13 | East Coweta | 24–9 |
| December 21 | Brookwood | 28–7 |

## 2003 Parkview Panthers (13-2)

| August 30 | Dacula | 21–3 |
|---|---|---|
| September 12 | Brookwood | LOST 35–21 |
| September 19 | Berkmar | 28–0 |
| September 26 | Collins Hill | 31–17 |
| October 3 | Central Gwinnet | 35–13 |
| October 10 | Meadowcreek | 70–7 |
| October 17 | Norcross | 29–14 |
| October 24 | Oconee County | 45–14 |
| October 31 | Shiloh | 38–16 |
| November 14 | Dacula | 31–0 |

| November 21 | Campbell | 20–13 |
| --- | --- | --- |
| November 28 | Chattahoochee | 3–0 |
| December 5 | Newnan | LOST 20–14 |

## BRINGING IT BACK TO WOMACK

The Statesboro Blue Devils went 2-3 in title games under two different head coaches in the decade. Buzz Busby's power running game was introduced in 1999, and he made three visits in a five-year period to start the run. After a shutout by Columbus-Shaw in 2000, he went undefeated himself in '01, putting up 51 points against Dalton in a 38-point blowout at Womack Field 51–13. He returned for another chance at a title in 2003 but lost to an equally disciplined Marist team, 21–6. Steve Pennington took over as head coach in 2004, but he lost in another home game in Statesboro to Warner Robins High 34–13. Realizing, perhaps, the bad luck their home stadium was giving them (but in reality moving to a larger venue to accommodate all the fans wanting to come), the 2005 game was moved to Paulsen Stadium on the Georgia Southern University campus. A twenty-nine-yard Josh Rich field goal was good with seven seconds left to give the Blue Devils a 13–10 win over Northside–Warner Robins.

But the Eagles would get their own measure of championship success with their own run in AAAA and AAAAA. If you ask Mike Davis, however, he thinks the genesis of the success started in the last chapter. "Going back, I think the win over Lowndes in 1997 turned everything around for Northside," the Eagles play-by-play announcer admits. "They were number one in the world at the time. There was an eight-minute drive where the fans actually got on Coach Nix for not passing the ball. All he did was pound the ball on the right side that whole time. Sheldon Hogan scored with about a minute to go for the win."

That 13–10 win sent Lowndes home and started one of the best rivalries in the state at present. If you look over the last fifteen years, one school has had to go through the other to get to a title shot.

Northside got its semifinals appearance in the 2001 season, but from 2005 to 2009, the Nix-coached teams showed up in game fifteen four times. That loss to Statesboro in 2005 lent itself to back-to-back 15-0 seasons and title wins against Marist (for the school's first-ever crown) and Ware County—one at McConnell-Talbert Stadium in Warner Robins and the other in Waycross.

But the run meant so much more to the Northside community.

# Winning It with Chris

Christopher Aurez Johnson played one year of varsity football for Northside. In the summer of 1995, he was diagnosed with acute lymphoblastic leukemia (ALL). Johnson became a source of strength for other children fighting cancer in central Georgia as he himself faced aggressive treatment cycles, a round of remission and an angrier round two with ALL. He eventually became a spokesperson for kids with cancer at the Children's Hospital in Macon, and his work with the Jay's Hope Foundation led to the single largest day of African American bone marrow registrants in middle Georgia history.

Chris went to games with his parents, Pat and Ovie, and was on the sidelines—whether it was standing or in a wheelchair—whenever possible to be part of the Eagles family.

Chris died in June 2007 due to complications from his chemotherapy treatments.

Coach Nix established the Christopher A. Johnson Champion in Life scholarship in his name through the Children's Miracle Network. According to the Tubman Institute, Nix eulogized Chris at his memorial service, saying that "Chris's legacy will live a long time and if you knew Chris, you know that Chris would do ANYTHING to help others."

The team continued its salute and dedication to Chris the following season. In the semifinal against Tucker at the Georgia Dome, Joe Scott filled in admirably for the injured Marques Ivory at quarterback after Ivory had broken his leg a month before. Up 28–7 at the half, Tigers head coach Franklin Stephens admitted in his interview on statewide television that he was still a little scared: "It's scary because everything is going our way. The question is, 'How can we keep momentum?'"

As it turns out, Northside grabbed the momentum, putting an immobile Ivory in at quarterback in the second half. Ivory threw touchdown passes to Kevyn Cooper for 69 yards in the third and 82 yards in the fourth. He finished by completing eleven of sixteen for 293 yards and three scores in a 31–28 win that set up the finals match-up against Ware County. Some of the team members wore orange "96" numbers, memorializing Chris, over their hearts for the game. Ivory, one of Johnson's best friends, said he knew Chris was watching over them. But they had to go one more week.

The championship game was just the way Gators head coach Dan Ragle wanted it—a battle of field position, tough defense and working the clock. The Eagles came out for the second half of a 7–6 game by walking around a breakthrough banner remembering Chris and carrying a portrait of him out onto the field. As the schools headed to the fourth quarter, every Northside fan held up a "96" placard to show support for the Johnsons.

A play not used since fall practice, a direct snap halfback pass from Tijuan Green to Nick Bass, gave the Eagles their second title, 20–14.

## AMERICUS BEFORE THE SUMTER

Head Coach Erik Soliday put an exclamation point on the Panthers' success in the first two years of the decade by having his own back-to-back titles over Washington-Wilkes in 2000 and Early County in 2001. Americus quarterback Robert Johnson set the single-season passing mark with 3,263 yards for the AA school. Almost half of those yards went to John Harris with 1,578. Washington-Wilkes tailback Daccus Turman grabbed the other record for the year as he ran for 3,172 yards, knocking Herschel Walker's Johnson County feats to second all-time. After the 2003 season, however, Sumter County High School merged with Americus High to form Americus-Sumter. The new version of the Panthers has only had one winning season since—in 2010.

Oh, about that Parkview Panthers streak…

Buford High School seemed to be right on Parkview's heels for both championship numbers and consecutive wins. Three state championships were put in Head Coach Dexter Wood's dossier along the way, and he appeared in a fourth in 2004, when he eventually lost to Charlton County.

"You don't know you're going through it thinking you're a part of history," he admits. "It is something magnificent and, therein, the reason it happens. We were able to set a pattern of a 'one-game only' focus."

One of those team stats is 47-0. But one game still sticks in his mind more than others. "The group of seniors that graduated in 2003 finished 58-2," and as Wood says that, he is still amazed. "I still remember the last time they lost—December 21, 2000, to Commerce. I sometimes regret that I couldn't teach these kids, or show them, how to deal with failure. They simply haven't failed. After the Commerce game, they were totally devastated. We were consoling them in the locker room. They had never experienced that before. I never got to teach that lesson to these kids—to get up when you get knocked down. It's a great problem to have."

And it was a program that went 118-17 when Dexter Wood was head coach and CEO of Buford Football. "There was a part of you that had to represent the 2001 team, the 2002 team and 2003 team. You've done that mighty well, and you've sealed the deal. Ya'll are to be commended for that," Wood admitted to a crowd of a few hundred in the south end zone after the game. "I know a lot of you were a part of those teams, and you're excited about what it means to all these people. I'm overwhelmed of this support, and what it means to our community."

His daughter Rachel had made the trip along with her husband, Jeff. Dexter's son Ryan stood to his father's right as he was having his impromptu roast.

Dexter said, "I don't understand sometimes how a person can be so blessed. These were the ones there when I was a youngster and didn't know what I was doing. Without their support, I'd be nothing." He then hugged his wife, Martha, and received a plaque that referred to the team as undefeated in 2001, uncontested in 2002, untouchable in 2003 and 2-0 in 2004.

Martha admits:

> *What he did was sweet and really meaningful to me. He's always done that with family—drawing them in like that, building us up and giving credit where it's due. He's always been good about paying compliments. They're always sincere and never cheap. He knows the sacrifices that go into making things a success. And with him, it's all part of being humble. His character has driven him all his life, and God has honored that in the end.*

Current Buford head coach Jess Simpson says:

> *Dexter is always someone who wants to share the credit. He wanted to make that ceremony have that tone to it. It's who he is. He is a class act. I don't know anybody else like him. He's talked to me before about this. He said that God gives you an equipping grace to do certain things. Being with him for thirteen years, I can't ever imagine having those gifts and how he's able to articulate and define certain things. Football is football. But it really is about people. That's where he is so special.*

And Jess admits that someday, the win against Union County may be a special one, too.

## ANOTHER WALKER RUNS THE BALL

One of those obvious reasons Buford was successful was someone named Darius Walker. Walker was a tailback who simply could not be caught more games than most. He would break records along the way—one of them previously held by Herschel Walker. At the summer scrimmage, the coaching staff would stack the deck against him. It would be the defense playing against the first-team offense or the offense against the first-team defense. Another Dexter Wood approach would be to set up either side to fail in practice just to see how the teams would respond.

Dexter says, "They would wonder, 'What is Coach doing here?' I would do that early in the year just to see how morale would be established. I could do it in a scrimmage or a drill, and tell someone they're not starting just 'because.' Always keep them guessing. It was a way to tell them that they were going to do it together. It's not about you, or you, or you."

In football, you can easily get injured and lose a career. You can lose a starting spot and have to fight for work. It's how you respond, persevere and grow. Football will teach you those things—as well as how to handle success and special athletes that come along every blue moon or so.

"I knew in his eighth-grade year that Darius was special," Dexter says.

Darius had good parents who kept his head in the right place all the time. He had even played in that state championship game as a freshman. But Wood never figured that it would get to the level of success or attention it eventually did over time. Darius was seen as articulate, humble and educated—the perfect ambassador for Buford Wolves football. Darius and another Wood player, Marietta High School quarterback Eric Zeier, became the first most recognizable names at the next levels of football.

The 2003 season was Darius's senior season, and there was talk that he would break the single-season touchdown record in the state semifinal against Decatur. But Dexter Wood was more focused on "this week" than records. As it got later in the game, Darius hadn't been in the end zone enough yet. Fans were getting itchy. The media was anticipating history. Dexter Wood was trying to call plays to win a game "this week."

Dexter admits:

*I wish I could be in a game calm enough to figure something like that out. I know in the fourth quarter he [Darius] hadn't scored. In the first or second quarter, I forget, Zach Smith had caught a pass in the flat, and he really had made it in the end zone. But they marked him down at the six-*

*inch line. I wasn't thinking about a record then. I was thinking, "Zach deserves this." I have to send in a play in ten seconds from the sideline, and, "What am I going to do?" Hand the ball seven yards back just to go six inches forward?*

There were offensive game plans where Darius would get the ball and try to score from the five- or six-yard line and inside. But in the Decatur semifinal, there had been five or six different scorers. Darius didn't have any big runs in that game, and Dexter admits that the semifinal was one of his poorest efforts of the year. The game is played at the Georgia Dome on statewide television. The old Astroturf had been replaced with the newer SprinTurf. That creation has ground-up automobile tires mixed in with garbage bags as a playing surface. When you run on it, the tire shards kick up, end up in your shoes and can make running very difficult—even painful.

"I think Darius ran out of aggravation that day," Dexter says. "He had the stuff all in his face after our first possession, and the look on his face was one like, 'Let's get this game over with.'"

They did—and won another state title.

"The great thing is," Jess Simpson admits, "every kid on our teams has a role. It's not all Darius Walkers. It's average Joes that buy into the process and make a play in the biggest game of the year. And when you see a kid graduate, one who, maybe, didn't have any support at home? Those are the people and the relationships that make this so special. When we do it together as we have, that's what makes it so much fun.

"It's about enjoying the journey. You remember the average players who played well and the good players who played great."

## WHERE'S CAMDEN COUNTY?

The answer is Region 3, down in the southeast corner of the state and the home of the King's Bay Submarine Base. Kingsland is a military town with a fairly fluid population, but under Head Coach Jeff Herron, the double-blue Wildcats have become a national name in a very short time. It took a win at Valdosta to start the headlines in 2003, and one key play is remembered by the town and Coach Herron:

*We had called a play right before that—"Right Trips, 29 Waggle Switch." The split end was open and our quarterback, Emmanuel Bacon, didn't see him. Either we had screwed up blocking or the quarterback got outside of where he was supposed to be. Unfortunately, it had become a topic among my coaches right after the play. My offensive coordinator, who had come with me from Oconee County, and my offensive line coach, who had come with me from Oconee County, are on headsets arguing over whose fault it was. It was the heat of the battle and those things happen all the time.*

*But here we are. There's fifteen seconds left in the half and they're going at each other. I'm looking at Slats* [Coach Greg Slattery] *and I'm going, "What are we thinking? What are we thinking?" and he's arguing with* [Coach Scott] *Carmichael. And they're arguing going back and forth. I'm looking at him and I'm looking at him going, "SOMEBODY, HELP ME OUT HERE!" And I finally grabbed* [split end] *D.J.* [Jones] *and told him to run it again. This time we blocked it the right way. Emmanuel threw the perfect pass, and we scored. It's one of those things nobody would believe. It's probably one of the biggest plays we've ever had here, and that's what happened.*

"Winning the title brought the people in Camden County together," Frank Smith, one of the biggest Camden County backers of all time, says. "We all just went crazy. You know? That's the first time since the school was integrated that we had won a state title in anything. If you put anything on a T-shirt about that championship team you couldn't keep enough of them printed before they were all snapped up." Bunche High winning a state title had been the only county representation until that Wildcat title. That spans roughly a thirty-year range.

Camden County followed that title up with two more, as well as finishing the 2008 and 2009 seasons with national rankings. The Wildcats won the 2008 AAAAA title against an upstart Peachtree Ridge team that came into the title game as a four-seed and ran the table to get to week fifteen. One of Jeff Herron's friends and former assistants, Bill Ballard, was on the other sideline.

Herron admits:

*We were kinda in control for most of the game. But then they broke off that huge ninety-four-yard touchdown run. That changed the momentum of the whole thing. And then we hit an eighty-five-yard bomb on third down to tie it back up. We drive again and score on fourth down, but then I made a stupid call on another drive on a first or second down and* that *almost cost us a chance to win.*

Greg Slattery and Jeff Herron, the Camden County brain trust. *Courtesy Bob Dandeneau.*

*But then, midway through the fourth, I think we finally had it in control.
It was a great feeling to win, but the year was different. We didn't have a lot
of close games, but it was a culmination of a great year. In 2008, we were
coming off a disappointing loss in '07. Our nucleus was coming back, so I
thought the year would be a good one. The trip to Hoover was a great trip
for the kids and a great environment. The semifinal was a great trip and a
great environment, and then the final was at the Georgia Dome.*

*Those kids were driven that year.*

And then the double blue followed that up with a win at the Georgia
Dome against Northside–Warner Robins—a game that quickly fell into
Camden's hands, and they didn't let go of it all night long.

Herron recalls:

*It was a strange game. It was our strangest championship. We were
struggling early in the year. A lot of people had doubts when we started out
1-2. People were telling us that we weren't worth a dime. But things got
a little better, and then a little better, and then a little better. That one was
more satisfying, and it was a different feeling. We were going, "How far
can we ride this?"*

*And in the final, it took only three plays for us to get up 14 points. Then, it took another two plays on a short drive for us to get up 20 points. You're up 21–0, and you felt like the breath had run out of you. We were still scared, and you felt like you couldn't relax. But as the game went on, you could kind of stand around a little bit and go, "We've got this one."*

# LaGrange Wins Three of Four

The AAA class is regarded, top to bottom, as the toughest place to win a title in the state. The personalities and experience of the LaGrange coaching staff under Steve Pardue gave the rest of the field headaches in one four-year span, starting in 2001.

"If we're up 35–0 in a game, Coach David Traylor is going crazy," Pardue says. "I tell him that if he doesn't calm down, I'm going to take his headset away from him. In a game like Cedartown, he is the calmest person. And he gives me a calming effect."

"This was the one time," Coach Traylor remembers about the title game in Polk County, "that I was sitting outside thinking that I was really cold. Everything is going wrong in that first half. And if I'm thinking, 'I'm cold,' that's not good. Things were just not going our way."

Cedartown scored 19 points in the second quarter. The Grangers were down 19–7 at the half.

Coach Donnie Branch recalls:

*Remember, LaGrange hadn't been in a championship game since 1991, so we were really excited. At the half, I got on our guys really hard. They hadn't been playing like they had the last seven weeks before then. I challenged our best four guys to upgrade their play. We got after it pretty good.*

*We knew if we slowed them down in the second half, we could punch it through. We had been moving the ball on them. We just hadn't scored.*

But they had to keep fighting uphill after Patrick Higgins fumbled a punt. "I told P.T., 'Keep your head up,'" Pardue says. "I said, 'You're gonna make a big play! We need you!' He was really down after that punt. But I had tremendous confidence in our guys."

Kenny Moore, the offensive line coach at the time, was even more confident. Pardue could hear him over his headset telling everyone else,

"This is gonna be great! We're going to win a state championship. And we're going to come from behind to do it!"

"I was at a practice at the University of Georgia," Pardue remembers. "The tight end coach, Greg Atkins, yells at me, 'Hey, Pardue! Look at this!' It was a play they called 'Go-Switch.' The outside receivers run inside, and the inside receivers run outside. I liked it, and we ran it then."

Adrian Griffin caught the pass from Blake Mitchell and got the ball to the seven-yard line.

"At the end of the game, we're within a touchdown or so," Traylor says. "I was telling the guys that if we got one more opportunity, we have the chance to win. I was asking, 'Lord, just let us have one more chance to win it.' We stuck it in the end zone somehow."

Patrick Higgins was just the guy to get his body in the right position to catch the ball and keep it away from the defender. Blake could always throw the fade really well, and that play was the Grangers' ace in the hole.

The fade route became the third-down play. They'd run the option on fourth down now if they had to make another shot at it.

The fade got the score on the board for the lead. The first touchdown of the year had been a fade route from Blake Mitchell to Patrick Higgins. So was the last one.

But you had to be in seats above the bottom row of stands to see it since they were below field level. You couldn't see anything otherwise on the visitors' side of the field. Blake ran the option into the end zone for the two-point conversion. Those relatives who stayed inside the stadium for the Pardues included a lot of people who came down from Kentucky to see title number one.

"Their visitors' sideline was so small," Pardue says. "With twelve seconds left, I was trying to get everybody back so we didn't get a penalty. I was yelling, 'GET BACK!' I actually shoved one of our team doctors. I didn't remember I did until a few days later, and I called to apologize. He was laughing, telling me that he understood."

What a lot of people may not know is the Grangers played the final play with only ten players on the field. A communications problem put the team in a different "prevent" defense than the one they thought they were in.

"I couldn't get on the field," Steve's wife, Pam, says. "I couldn't get to the gate, and security wasn't letting anyone on. So my brother and my dad picked me up, put me over the fence and onto the track. I couldn't find him [Steve]. It took forever! But when I finally found him, you can't believe it happened to you. It's a mile marker in your life."

"We enjoyed the Christmas holidays," Steve says with a smile, understanding the understatement.

It was a defining moment for Coach Pardue and the rest of the staff. But few people remember that he had to beat a Hart County team two weeks earlier in a match-up of number one versus number two." The town of Hartwell was another one of those great high school environments that Pardue always enjoys going to along the lines of Cairo, Gainesville, Forsyth (Mary Persons) or Fort Valley (Peach County). The Hart County students knew all the players' names for appropriate jeering. But LaGrange played as good a half as they could and won 49–0.

After that game, it was a semifinal against North Forsyth that set up the game in Cedartown.

Pardue recalls:

> We won 35–13, but it was only something like 9–6 at the half. It was our first time in the Georgia Dome. You have to get used to that atmosphere. I couldn't hear with twenty thousand people in there. I don't know how you can hear with seventy-five thousand. Normally, our pre-game routine is set to the minute. At 6:12, we're doing this. At 6:15, we're doing this. There at the Dome, you're guaranteed thirty minutes to warm up. It might be more. It might not. We're looking up at the clock, cutting five-minute segments to three.
>
> We ran in to the locker room. We said, "Amen!" I don't even think we got in a full prayer.

But the philosophy of practicing offense, defense and special teams equally, putting your best players on defense, not turning the ball over, playing hard, hitting the other guy and not beating yourself turns into titles more often than not.

Some people will see games that are low-scoring and see works of art. Others will see cures for insomnia. It's a thing of beauty if you know what to look for.

"Remember Charles Flowers when he coached at Shaw?" Pardue asks. "If he got a lead on you, it was over."

And the next year? Pardue remembers:

> That week, we put in another special play. Our quarterback Thad Todd was supposed to fake the sweep, fake the counter, hold the ball in his stomach and walk backward.

*I told Thad, "You gotta trust me. If you sell it, it will be the play of the Dome. It will be all over TV. People will talk about it." Demoreo Ford was supposed to sell his block and then slip by his man. Thad made a great fake and throw. It was an unbelievable catch—all on a first-and-22 for a 7–0 lead. Ben Higgins hit a 50-yard field goal for the last play of the half. We were an offensive team from then on.*

Another championship game followed—this time in Fort Valley. And there's something about LaGrange and the weather at championship games. They think the cold helped them out again. Three of the team's defensive players, including Tray Blackmon and Robert Ramey, didn't even practice until Thursday of championship week. They wore casts during the week, went to physical therapy and the coaches hoped and prayed that those kids wouldn't get hurt. The casts were cut off in time for the games on the weekend.

"On paper, I think they [Peach County] were two to three touchdowns better than we were," Traylor says. "But there's Steve saying we were going to win the game. He wasn't exactly sure how, but we were."

"We played WaCo on Friday and stayed around to scout the other game," Pardue says. "I was spent, but I was in the suite they give you inside the Georgia Dome. I was talking to [Thomas County Central head coach] Ed Pilcher most of the game. I looked at them and said, 'Golly, they're big.' But I didn't know how big they were until we got there on the field."

A friend of Steve's was looking at Peach County's players. He told Steve that he had seen two guys leaning on the goal posts. Steve knew they weren't all that tall. Or did he?

"They were in all black. I looked at them. Then I looked at us. I looked at them again. And I decided not to look again. I might get scared. I told our guys before the game, 'Well, I think we'll get under their pads.' They were monsters."

The Grangers went out as ready as they could. Their offensive line coach, David Pleasants, had coached at Peach, so there was a little familiarity in the Trojans' way of thinking. They put in a running play that worked twice—once to the one-foot line and another for a score through the air. Peach drove but eventually self-destructed.

Branch's defense, filled with juniors, knocked another ball loose on the goal line against Peach County in the title game. Conventional wisdom with that particular team—at least on the defensive side of the ball—was that once the Grangers had a lead, the game was over. It didn't matter what the size of the lead was. They were, admittedly, scared of Peach quarterback A.J. Bryant, so LaGrange worked hard on containing him in the pocket. But Pardue was confident in their ability to get to him. When the Trojans' high-powered offense went to a four wide-receiver set, LaGrange countered with Trey Blackmon as a speed-rushing end. He finished with a handful of sacks on the night.

An intentional grounding call in the end zone gave LaGrange a 16–7 lead late in the game. Peach had to try an onside kick to get the ball back. It failed, and another title was heading back to Troup County.

The game was over. Peach hadn't played well. LaGrange had. And they got a few breaks along the way.

"I think we got every ounce of what the players had that year," Branch says. "It's amazing what those kids did. They refused to realize their limitations."

And things find a way of evening out along the span of a season.

"When we won in Cedartown, I just broke down," Pardue says. "But after we won at Peach County, I was just sitting there going, 'Is this really happening?' I was giggling. I wasn't emotional or anything. No one thought we'd win that one."

"We were totally out-athleted," Athletics Director Jay Russell admits now. "We were outmanned. But we got after their tails."

Pardue talked to his quarterback, Thad Todd, during a late timeout. Their relationship would be a special one from that moment on. Pardue says:

> He was like me at the Cedartown game. He had been Blake Mitchell's backup for two years. I didn't have Thad play ninth-grade football since I didn't want to waste any quarters that I could have him play at the varsity level. He understood the offense as well.
>
> This is a football town. I know the barbershops criticize me, the players and everybody else. I'm sure they criticized Thad's ability to lead us. And he lost it when the game was over.

And when you go back to back, it's a very small group to be included in. LaGrange historian Scott Sickler admits:

> We've had a plethora of great teams at LaGrange from the times of Coach Amos Teasley, Bernie Moore, legendary Oliver Hunnicutt, Gary Guthrie and Steve Pardue, but you don't like to compare them as state champs. However, when you stop and think about it a minute, it's a nice problem to have, isn't it? I've only seen LaGrange football from 1979 to present and

*I believe the 2004, nationally ranked in six polls, 15-0 and AAA state champion team was the best in school history for one reason—the most complete, super fast, super physical, intimidating defense we've ever had.*

*LaGrange was so good in '04 that it wasn't a question of if LaGrange was going to win but by how many they wanted to win by and how many opposing players would get knocked out of games. That '04 bunch were kamikazes.*

The Grangers went 87-8 from 2000 to 2005.

There's something else that saw every play of that run: a portrait of Coach Hunnicutt that hung over Coach Pardue's desk in his office. Pardue admits:

*You look back, and he was the one that got all the history going. He stayed around after he retired. He even lived across the street from the school when I first came here. He would come over at 9:00 a.m., go home, come back, eat lunch, come back for practice, walk around the field, take a half-lap around the track and come back again.*

*It was really special to know him later in life. I would take him to the Touchdown Club banquets in Atlanta, and everyone mobbed him.*

*But the picture above the desk? He's keeping an eye on me. It used to be in the front office. They were changing things around, and they asked me what to do with the picture. I said, "I know what we're going to do with it. I've got a place for it." It's going to go with me when I leave here, so they better check.*

Pardue loved hanging around Hunnicutt and listening to his many stories. He felt guilty when Hunnicutt's sons would thank him for spending time with their father, because Pardue enjoyed it so much. Coach Pardue also admits it was a tough time when the coach passed.

If you ask older coaches who they think of when you say "LaGrange High," they'll talk about Coach Oliver Hunnicutt. The younger coaches will mention Steve Pardue. He sees it as nothing but a compliment. "But I hope he's looking down," he closes, "and is proud of the way we're doing things here."

# HAWKINSVILLE'S FIRST IN A LONG TIME

The night before the 2003 title game between Hawkinsville and Lincoln County, the Hawkinsville team left town to catch *The Last Samurai*. The movie's ideas about discipline and "fighting your heart out" sunk in. But the team was sequestered inside the field house on game day. Normal circumstances would tell you to open the doors, let the players sit on the patio and let the experience sink in. But Lincoln County tailgating started early on Saturday in the parking lot, and the coaches wanted focus. The general admission was packed by 4:30 p.m. for a kickoff ninety minutes away.

"It looked like Woodstock," Lee Campbell remembers. "People were coming from everywhere. I had to go back in the field house and I just started laughing. I said to the coaches, 'You need to go look at this.' It was so good for the town to host the game. We got a standing ovation when we went out to warm up. Our receivers were catching balls and the crowd was going crazy."

The stadium holds close to three thousand people. Estimates were all over the place, from five to ten thousand people watching. That is a little farfetched. Okay, a lot farfetched. Campbell thinks it was more like six thousand. It was still the largest crowd Bobby Gentry Stadium had ever seen. One of Lee's assistants, Cam Black, had talked about this idea a few years before—Lee Campbell beats Larry Campbell.

And, sure enough, it happened—18–8.

Lee doesn't get too excited after big plays or big game wins. He always wants to come across as someone who has been there, done what he needed to do to win and is looking forward to returning very soon. He still carries a key chain that his mentor, Coach Jeff Caldwell, gave him in high school that carries his philosophy: "Do It with Class."

"To have my dad here meant a lot," he admits. "After the game was over, there were a lot of people on the field. My wife, Alicia, was one of the first ones I looked for. Everyone is sticking microphones and tape recorders at you. I just said a few things and I ran down to where he was. My aunt and sister brought him down. To have him there was really special."

He thinks the win excited his father enough to where he wanted to walk into the center of all the hoopla. His father walks every day, but this was an extra dose of momentum for him. Wins do that. Special wins do that much more. Especially coming from a son who feels that his father saved his life.

# CHARLTON'S RETURN

After appearing in nothing worse than the quarterfinals leading up to the 2003 season, Coach McWhorter's team put together a four-year run that was one of the better ones in state history—54-5-1, with four title appearances and three title wins in a row. As many as eighteen Charlton County athletes were part of that group that won three of four. The same quarterback, tailback and nucleus were successful as sophomores, juniors and seniors.

"You could make a list of things that could go wrong, and you don't need for them to happen," McWhorter says. "If one kid gets injured, you lose two starters. The biggest thing we went through was to say, 'Let's keep an eye on each other and not do anything stupid or foolish.'"

In 2004, the first title was payback for the previous year's loss to Buford with a 35–20 win behind quarterback Dwight Dasher, running back Lemuel Walker and wide receivers Justin Williams, David Pender and D.J. Donley. Dasher left Folkston as the team's all-time leading scorer, while Walker was the school's all-time touchdown leader. That group had played every sport imaginable or allowable since junior high and lost at nothing—specifically football and track—and had been competitive since kindergarten. At recess, the kids would all come back into school dirty and bleeding from playing so hard. These Indians were scared to death of losing and, frankly, didn't know how to do that. In McWhorter's mind, going to Buford, Calhoun and Dublin was the challenge the team needed.

McWhorter says:

> *It gave us another opponent—the trip. I had a motto: "Expect to win." But on game days, I had this mental highlight film going through my head where the opponent could do no wrong. The kids would look at me and go, "Coach, we got this." They were never nervous, and they were an amazing group of kids. I called them "characters with some character." They were fun to be around, and emotionally, they were more even-keeled than I was.*
>
> *It's more special to beat someone on their own field. When you travel and win, grown men just cry. You don't forget it soon after, and every year somehow you have a group of kids that bring it together and do it one more time.*

## LOWNDES STARTS ITS RUN

After Milt Miller's title in 1999, Randy McPherson came up from Florida and made sure that when everyone went into the "Concrete Jungle" (Martin Stadium) they knew that the Vikings' winning ways would continue.

Starting in 2004 as well, the Vikings went 29-1 in back-to-back title years. After an uncharacteristic 6-4 season in 2006, the third Class AAAAA title came in a monsoon against North Gwinnett for another 14-1 season.

Lowndes play-by-play announcer Wes James admits:

> *In 2004, I don't think everyone was expecting even the run the team had through the region. When we got to Parkview and the players got off the bus and we walked through the fence line, all you hear is that Guns N' Roses song "Welcome to the Jungle." But to beat Ware County the way we did and then go up to the Big Orange Jungle? They ended up as a real powerhouse that year. Everyone was talking about them having problems stopping Caleb King. That was the general consensus. And when they did, it was the end of it right there.*

That 17–14 win on the road, coupled with the 49–7 win at home, gave the Vikings their back to back. But there would be far more to celebrate in '07—even as the first game of the year was a loss to Harrison 9–0 in the Corky Kell Kickoff Classic. They would run the table from there and carry another piece of school history with them into the next decade: the Vikings have not lost to cross-town rival Valdosta since 2003, and that streak includes a 57–15 win in 2009 that caused the *Valdosta Daily Times* to change its headline from "Vikings Sack Wildcats" to "Wildcats Sack Coach," as Rick Tomberlin's short tenure at Valdosta High came to a sudden end after the season.

## A PEACH OF A GIG

Rance Gillespie was given the head coaching job at Peach County in 2001 after a two-year stint at Banks County in northeast Georgia. His two years at Banks were nothing to write home about—going 5-15—but his time with the Trojans showed the growth and restoration of the program. During his third year, the team made it to the finals. But in 2005 and 2006, his teams went back to back as champs and were very different.

Gillespie remembers:

> One year we had two kids who were very talented, but we had just graduated a group of kids that was probably, as a group, the most talent that I've ever had. We were 11-2 and got beat in game thirteen in 2004. They all walked across the stage and graduated. The next year, we started the season 0-3 and said it's going to be a struggle. But our kids were a lot of fun to be around and they went out and went to work each and every day and just gelled.
>
> We had two really good football players and we got on a little run. And if you don't think that momentum during the season is important, it's a great example to support that theory. It's not always talent. Some things have to fall in line for you. Your team has to gel a little bit for you, and more than anything, you've got to have good character. We had a good character football team that year. I didn't have to come to work and wonder whether or not they were going to be at school.
>
> The first one [championship] I remember driving in to the stadium at Dougherty and they hadn't opened the stadium yet. The lines were unbelievable, and that's a special feeling—driving into the stadium seeing all those people. As we came out to warm up, there were people sitting all around the rock. I had never seen that many people sitting at Hugh Mills Stadium before. As we're coming out, I keep hearing this "tink…tink…" and one of my kids is flinching. I said, "What is it?" He said, "Coach, they're throwing pennies at us!"
>
> I don't think you'll ever forget the first time you round your sideline, and your home side sees you and they go bananas. It's a great, great feeling. As that game wound down, I still remember being anxious and it was 34–14 with two or three minutes left. It's kind of a surreal feeling of "What can go wrong now?"
>
> The next year we lost the two really good football players, and have even more of a complete football team in 2006. I can't say that I'm proud of one group more than the other. It was just really different.

## LINCOLN COUNTY IS STILL THERE

For Coach Campbell, a win in October 2002 for his 347th was all about the kids and showing respect for Dan Pitts—the hometown kid whose state record he had just broken. The win was supposed to happen in Commerce,

Larry Campbell has an .849 winning percentage since 1972. *Courtesy Mercer Harris,* Lincoln Journal.

but all the television cameras seemed to fire the Tigers up. It wasn't going to happen then. It had to wait for a home date.

Campbell admits:

> *I don't even compare myself in Xs and Os to him* [Pitts]. *He is the epitome of the finest high school coach of anybody at any level. I don't see myself as being the football coach that Dan Pitts was. He lived, ate and slept football. I do what it takes. I spend a lot of hours with it. But each year I try to spend more time doing other things—whether it's spending more time in church or visiting mom and dad more often.*
>
> "*But breaking his record? Maybe if it had been some jerk that I didn't like it would have been one thing, but breaking Dan Pitts's record? I would never put myself in the class of a Ray Lamb, a Dan Pitts or a Nick Hyder…the list goes on and on. I still don't put myself in their place with Xs and Os. I think I've been fortunate to work with great administrations. I think we run a good program with good assistants.*

# 2006: The Year of the Tie

In Clinch County, you went through the Pee-Wees, the Wee-Pees and the Midgets before you were a full-fledged Panther. You didn't start in football until the second grade back when Jim Dickerson was growing up, but now the kids are introduced to flags around their waists before what the bigger towns would call Pop Warner–aged football games.

A pass is intercepted and run back to the five-yard line of Hawkinsville. Clinch County runs a play that was supposed to be to the middle of the field. The tailback sees a gap to his left and runs that way. The quarterback, Lamar McKnight, has to spike the ball to stop the clock. The Panthers line up on the left hash mark for the spot. A few plays before, Boris Lee, the kicker, had hurt his ankle playing defense. The kick goes straight instead of the forty-five-degree angle to the right needed for the game-winner.

The kids had played over their heads all season long. Three- and four-year starters like Lee, McKnight and Jarvis Henderson were an influence for all the younger players. When these three—and others like them who were widely respected—spoke about what was to be done, the rest fell in line.

Clinch County color commentator Eric Lutz admits:

> *When it ended like it did, I thought it was fitting. Everyone went totally silent. They were so spent emotionally. Everyone was gearing up for overtime, and the kids all looked like they lost. They say a tie is like kissing your sister. I never had a sister, but for that game, it was the proper way to finish. The Hawkinsville people were relieved. We all feel the same way. And the Hawkinsville people will say the same thing. This was the best game we've ever seen.*

"I was a bundle of nerves that game in Hawkinsville," Head Coach Jim Dickerson's wife, Kristi, admits. "On the way up there my momma said that she had heard that they could tie. I said, 'No, that isn't the way it was going to be. One of you is going to be the champion. That's not it. That's not right.' And I'll be dog-gone if that wasn't what happened."

In the last two minutes of the game, play-by-play man Len Robbins and Lutz were wondering, "What happens if it ends in a tie?" Len thought he remembered reading somewhere that if the game was tied that was how it would end.

"I was scared to say that on the air, though," Len says laughing. "I think Hawkinsville was scared to go into overtime, and we were just as scared. Not in the sense of being afraid, but in the idea that we both thought the game could end on one of those big plays. Me? I was petrified there would be one of those long passes for the win."

Even Jim Dickerson didn't realize the game could end in a tie.

Clinch (13-1-1) and Hawkinsville (14-0-1) ended the Class A championship tied 14–14, the first shared football championship since Lakeside and Kendrick were declared co-champions in Class AAA in 1991 and the fourth overall. Georgia High School Association regulations don't allow overtime in football title games.

"I heard Coach [Jim Dickerson] said it was like kissing your sister," said Hawkinsville coach Lee Campbell of his Clinch counterpart. "But it's better than kissing your brother."

Hawkinsville's twenty-nine-game winning streak became a thirty-game unbeaten streak. With the tie, the school claimed its fifth state title, while Clinch had its fourth.

By the end of the decade, Clinch was back chasing another title at the Georgia Dome against Savannah Christian. The year before, quarterback Trey Dorsey had been stopped five yards short from playing in the 2009 final when he was tackled as time expired. Dorsey admitted the play is "something that you think about the rest of your life." He got his chance at retribution and closure.

The Panthers won 24–14 for the school's fifth and Dickerson's second for a town of just under three thousand people. Football championships mean just as much, if not more, to schools and towns this size. Dickerson admits:

*We feel like football is a large part of who we are and what we have. It means an awful lot to our kids and our community. You hate to say that it's all we have, but it's a lot of what we have here. These kids grow up wanting to be a part of it and they realize there's only a window of opportunity so big. They really try to go out with everything they have. We feel like every Friday night, they're living life to the fullest and doing what they want to do.*

## FAMILY HISTORY IS MADE

In the 2000s on two fronts, Georgia had some of the same names etched in the record books. The first came with the Campbell brothers—Hawkinsville's Lee and Peach County's Chad. When Chad went an undefeated 15-0 in

2009 to give Peach County a title in a win over Gainesville, he became part of the first brother duo to win trophies by mid-December.

When did Chad find out he had made history? After the game itself, as he had never known about the distinction. The Trojans broke up a 2-point conversion after time had expired to preserve the 13–12 win.

And when Sandy Creek High's Fighting Patriots became AAAA champs that same season, Head Coach Chip Walker joined his dad, Rodney, in the father-son category as champs. Chip (as in "chip off the ol' block") even won a title in two separate classifications the following year with a AAAA win.

"I may be the only coach that got to coach him in high school," Rodney admits, "have him coach with me as an assistant and then see him win a state championship. That's as big a thrill as I could ever wish for."

"That's a special honor," Chip says in return. "Something to have happen like that? That's something that they can't take away from you. It's a big deal." And now that both Mary Persons and Sandy Creek are in AAA, there could possibly even be a father squaring off against a son for the Georgia title.

# But Buford Rules AA

Again—with four titles in a row tying West Rome for consecutive crowns, and they'll have a chance to set the new record in 2011.

But the streak didn't start without some change at the top as Dexter Wood became athletic director, leaving the head coaching keys in the very capable hands of Jess Simpson after the 2004 title game loss to Charlton County.

"Sometimes you just know when it's time to do something and the time for me to step down is now," Wood told the *Gwinnett Daily News* at the time. "I was having a little trouble this year being energized. The program may have reached a stagnant point and I think some new blood so to speak will help everybody," he said. "It was definitely a great time of my life and I wouldn't trade anything in the world for that."

All Simpson and the Wolves staff have done is go 58-2 since—with a 32-game win streak on the front end and two 13-game win streaks as part of the back end. It's the best ten-year run in state history. Only Lincoln County, which won seven of ten championships from 1985 to 1994, and Valdosta's seven in a ten-year stretch from 1960 to 1969 can match the Wolves.

"You look back on the last 10, 11 years and we've been blessed, probably a little lucky at times, but we're there because we've done things the right way,"

Buford High School head coach Jess Simpson.

Wood told the *Gwinnett Daily Post*'s Will Hammock after the 2010 season. "And the No. 1, main ingredient of it all is Jess Simpson."

All Simpson has done is go 82-4 in six seasons as Buford's head coach.

"This speaks to the vision Dexter Wood gave me in January of 1995, in the Marietta High School cafeteria when I was on lunch duty," Simpson said. "He had just stepped down [at Marietta] and he told me he was going to Buford and, 'Would you consider going with me? We're going to win some state championships there and build it the right way.' I followed him because I believed in him and his vision."

And that vision continues to this day.

# Chapter 8

# THE GEORGIA INTERSCHOLASTIC ASSOCIATION

O ne of the biggest regrets of legendary Cedartown head coach Doc Ayres was that he could not have his Bulldogs play with the athletes across town at the African American Cedar Hill High School. All he would do was shake his head when asked the question and wonder what his super team might have been like against the rest of the state. All Ayres could do was watch the Panthers, coached by Escue Rodgers, and look at what segregation was doing to the lives of student athletes.

The Panthers won a Georgia Interscholastic Association (the association for athletics in African American schools, sometimes referred to as the GIAA depending on the publication) championship every other year from 1951 to 1957. But the wins weren't without sacrifice or struggle—and even had assistant coaches writing up game reports for the local papers when their teams would win titles.

Take the 1955 win over Cook County, as reported by the *Cedartown Standard*:

> *The financial out-come of the game was not pleasing to either school. Total ticket sales, including advance and gate, were only $150. Expenses involved in sponsoring the game ran above $375.*
>
> *Besides the unpleasing results in the sale of tickets, the Panthers have had several severe injuries this year, creating large hospital and doctor bills in excess of $500 with no insurance on the players.*

The *Thomaston Times* from September 16, 1955, went into even more detail on how the Thomaston Training School (or Drake High) was trying to make ends meet:

> *In an effort to greatly help in the financing of their athletic and other school programs for the year, the Thomaston Training School has set as its goal an attendance of 2,000 at their opening home football game on October 7.*
>
> *In the past, the school has financed its program through raffles, lotteries, and popularity contests based on donations in addition to gate receipts from their games. However, the State Board of Education passed a law against such financing in July.*
>
> *School officials have contacted various civic organizations within the city for their aid in increasing the gate receipts at the opening game.*

Cedar Hill is one of those examples of "what might have been," as were the likes of Eureka High School, Boggs Academy, Fair Street and twenty-nine other recognized football champions from the Georgia Interscholastic Association. The fewer-than-two-hundred-member GIA ran from 1948 to 1971 and had three classifications: AA, A and B. While there are records and indications of teams representing high schools or college preparatory schools as far back as the 1920s with smaller, far-flung conferences, according to the Vanishing Georgia website associated with the state government and its archives system, the GIA is the only organized classes of champs and competition before integration started in the mid-1960s and was completed by 1970.

| YEAR | CLASS AA | CLASS A | CLASS B |
|---|---|---|---|
| **1948** | Washington (SW Atlanta) | | |
| **1949** | Washington (SW Atlanta) | Brooks | Union Normal Institute |
| **1950** | Spencer (Columbus) | Risley (Brunswick) | Tift County Industrial |
| **1951** | Washington (SW Atlanta) | Brooks | Cedar Hill |

| Year | Class AA | Class A | Class B |
|------|----------|---------|---------|
| 1952 | Spencer (Columbus) | Brooks | Tift County Industrial |
| 1953 | Howard (NE Atlanta) | Dasher | Cedar Hill |
| 1954 | Turner (Atlanta) | Center | Carver (Carrollton) |
| 1955 | Ballard-Hudson (Macon) | South Fulton | Cedar Hill |
| 1956 | Spencer (Columbus) | Center | Fair Street |
| 1957 | Risley (Brunswick) | Fair Street | Cedar Hill |
| 1958 | Washington (SW Atlanta) | Hunt | Elm Street |
| 1959 | Ballard-Hudson (Macon) | Douglass (Thomasville) | Wayne County Training |
| 1960 | Tompkins (Savannah) | Ralph Bunche (Woodbine) | |
| 1961 | Laney (Augusta) | Bryant (Moultrie) | Boggs Academy |
| 1962 | South Fulton (East Point) | Center | Boggs Academy |
| 1963 | South Fulton (East Point) | Pinevale (Valdosta) | Bruce Street (Lithonia) |
| 1964 | Howard (NE Atlanta) | Forrester (Alto) | Evans County |
| 1965 | Price (SE Atlanta) | Trinity (Decatur) | Boggs Academy/ Eureka (tie) |
| 1966 | Laney (Augusta) | Lemon Street (Marietta) | Eureka |
| 1967 | Spencer (Columbus) | Douglass (Thomasville) | Evans County |
| 1968 | Carver (Monroe) | | |
| 1969 | Houston (Perry) | | |

An interview with Dr. Eugene Walker talking about his Drake Yellow Jackets squad in *A History of Football in Upson County* seems to personify the era:

> *We didn't think of inferiority—we were just playing football in a system that wouldn't give us respect. We just tried to instill in our youth that if you were black, you had to be three times as good.*
>
> *We were better athletes, period. We could have beat them* [cross-town high school Robert E. Lee] *any day of the week.*

Walker also said that his time at Drake, while enjoyable, had its hardships. The one example he tells is wondering whether the buses his team traveled in would make it to their games in one piece or if the brakes would give out on the way there.

There was a lot of admiration between the athletes of white schools and black schools in the segregation era and a lot of game plan learning and sharing, even if they couldn't be teammates or rivals. Skipper Boone played high school football in Camden County but made a point to watch his counterparts at Ralph Bunche High.

Camden would play on Friday nights, and Bunche High's team would play on Saturdays on the same field. Whites couldn't come in on Saturdays, and blacks couldn't come in on Fridays.

"There was a fence at one end of the field," Skipper remembers as an old halfback in the T formation, "and the blacks would be there on Fridays. The whites would be there on Saturdays watching each other play. The high school was in Woodbine at the time. There was one small drugstore and after one of us would get a Coke and take it outside, we'd all discuss football." Skipper laughs and admits there was some talk of trading plays on the sidewalk.

The plays the Camden guys got from the Bunche players? "We never could figure out how to run them. They were always plays with a lot of razzle-dazzle, unbalanced lines, center on the end, spread out all over the field, but they won a state championship. My senior year, Ralph Bunche won a state championship."

Camden was a Class B school in those days, and as Skipper puts it:

> *Every stoplight in the county had a Class B school in it. We never had to travel more than fifty miles to play a game. This was before it wasn't unusual for a county like, say, Pierce to have more than one high school before consolidation of the school systems. Charlton County was a Class*

*B school back then, also. Glynn Academy was a AAAAA school then, and
we played their B team. Football was football, and it still is. The object
of the game is still the same—knock someone on their heinie and win the
ball game.*

And for the longest time, Bunche was known to be a state champ, but it
couldn't be proven because there was no record of their winning. And that's
only the beginning.

## EAST GEORGIA'S PANTHERS

Another example that seems to personify the time is the Boggs Academy
Panthers, located in the town of Keysville, twenty miles southwest of
Augusta. The three-time champs registered win-loss records of 3-1 in
1961, 2-0 in 1962 and 2-3-1 in 1965 under Head Coach Willie Coward.
Boggs was established as a boarding school by the Presbyterian Church
and offered three tracks for its students. Most students opted for the college
preparatory curriculum, but a number of students followed a business
curriculum, which prepared them for jobs after high school such as in
bookkeeping and office management. A third group, composed of a few
students who were from the local community, learned technical trades at
Boggs. The school was closed in 1984.

There were a handful of private schools in the state. Two were even
in the same town of Cordele—the Holsey-Cobb and Gillespie-Selden
Institutes. But the only school, public or private, that seemed to match
Boggs was Eureka out of Ashburn, as they tied Boggs 6–6 for the 1965
title. "Fox" Fields and "Slim" Walker connected for the only Tigers' score,
and there was a coin toss to determine who would take the trophy home.
Principal Hodge King won and declared that the banks in Ashburn would
get to house it. Coach John Dye was the only coach for Eureka on record
for seventeen seasons in the GIA era, with a win-loss record of less than
.500. Dye's repeat title in 1966 was a shutout of Boggs in Ashburn, and
these two seasons were the most successful Dye had in Turner County.
Workhorse Jackson was responsible for one of the scores in the 13–0
shutout as Boggs finished the year 7-4.

Moultrie-Bryant won its only Class A title also in 1961 in a 12–0 win over
Lemon Street High of Marietta. The crowd was announced at 3,500 by L.
"Pony" Jones, who was proud to write that A.F. Shaw finally had his first

title after twenty-seven years as a head coach. It was supposed to be a duel between the Rams' James Brown and the Hornets' Zelma Freeman, two of the most talented backs in the state for the year. But Brown's defensive skills were more needed with an interception that set up his rushing score on the night. A touchdown pass from Brown to Fred Daniels accounted for the other. Moultrie High, under Head Coach "Knuck" McCrary that year, went 7-2-1 and finished out of the playoff picture.

# MIDDLE GEORGIA:
# THE HOME OF LITTLE RICHARD AND OTIS REDDING

Ballard-Hudson Senior High School was built in 1949 as the only high school in Macon for African Americans in grades nine through twelve. The school represented the merger of two schools: Ballard High School, a private school with roots in Lewis High School, and Hudson High School, a public school. The campus of the new Ballard-Hudson Middle School is a historic site these days.

In 1955, Ballard-Hudson beat Howard twice (25–12 and 33–6) to win the AA title. In 1959, Ballard-Hudson knocked off Washington 14–7 as revenge for the 34–7 loss they had suffered to the Bulldogs the year before for their last title. Kenny Talton ran for a score, while Moses Herring threw a forty-five-yard touchdown to James Hill. The Maroons held Washington quarterback Leon Jamison, widely recognized as one of the best in the state at his position, to two completions and twenty yards of offense.

Over the years, schools became integrated, and the building went through several changes. The site last was home to Southeast High School, which closed in 2003. The new Ballard-Hudson Middle School was built and opened in January 2008.

In 1970, the same year a federal court required the integration of all public schools in Georgia, Ballard-Hudson Senior High School was reorganized and renamed. The grounds even have a historical marker noting the place in Georgia history that Ballard-Hudson holds. It was erected in 2004 by the Georgia Historical Society and the Historic Preservation Committee for the Ballard-Hudson Senior High School.

# Northeast Georgia

Fair Street's Tigers from Gainesville hold the distinction of being the only school in GIA history to get back-to-back titles, but in different classifications. The '56 title was in Class B, shutting out Evans County, while the '57 title was in Class A with a victory over Thomasville-Douglass, 13–7. The Tigers only gave up a total of 33 points in their 12-0 season, combining that with a 12-1 year before. A 1957 *Gainesville Times* article, while commending Gene Carrithers running and the coaching of E.L. Cabbell, noted that Fair Street's "strutting band presented an imaginative Christmas show during intermission that was complete even to a formation of a tree with blinking, colored lights."

"Little Gene," as he was called by *Times* sports editor Phil Jackson that day, took his 135-pound body for the game-winning score for the team's sixteenth straight victory and the state Class A trophy. Carrithers was key to both titles for Cabbell.

The Tigers were in position to play for the 1952 championship but decided against playing because the school couldn't afford it. They were in position to play Cedar Hill, but according to Principal C.W. Daniels in the *Gainesville Daily News*, the school "was already in the red financially…and it didn't seem that the attendance of the game would help the problem. If we had happened to win, it would have been impossible to finance a trip to the state championship in South Georgia."

Cedar Hill would then play Brooks High School, which was the African American counterpart for Brooks County High School in the southwest Georgia town of Quitman. They claim to have played in two national championship games by the start of the GIA. In the beginnings of the Class B rounds of the GIA, the "Fighting" Wildcats won three of the first four recorded titles, with Brunswick-Risley grabbing the one Brooks didn't in 1950. Once again, though, win-loss records are incomplete. Calvin Rutherford went 7-1-2, beating three Florida schools along the way in 1949 as schools looked to find competition where they could.

Here's how the *Quitman Free Press* described the win:

> *The Brooks Wildcats, coached by C.W. Rutherford, defeated the Thomaston Trojans in a game here on the QHS athletic field Thursday night by a score of 24–0. As a result of the victory the Brooks Wildcats are now state champions in Class A, this being the playoff game. The Quitman Negro team has gained a reputation throughout this section as being South Georgia*

*Champions for seven years out of the past nine years. This was the first time a statewide championship game was held.*

*A crowd estimated at 15000 saw the Wildcats trample the Trojans. Hundreds of white fans turned out for the game and the Brooks High team is supported by white and Negro fans.*

*The Thomaston game wound up a most successful season for the Brooks Wildcats. Out of 9 games they have lost only one, to Miami, Fla. They tied Ocala and Valdosta and defeated Lowndes County, Tallahassee, Brunswick, Waycross, Thomasville, and Moultrie.*

The other title years for Brooks were registered as 3-3 in 1951 and 2-1 in 1952.

# EAST POINT TURNS INTO SOUTH FULTON

In 1955, the orange and blue Lions that used to be known as East Point High School underwent a name change for the second time. That's when success came as well. Under Eldridge Hunter, the 1954 practice schedule was 2-0-1, but with Charles and Melvin Bell (and someone who would become a famous family name alumnus), South Fulton ran the table and immediately jumped from Class A to AA in time for basketball season—in their first year of competitive football, no less—beating Valdosta-Dasher in Valdosta 19–7.

The Lions had a week off before their championship game to prepare and even buried a version of "Mr. Dasher High" during a pep rally that week. Charles Bell ran and passed for a score in the game to put the Lions in the history books.

Creflo Dollar Sr. was also a starter on that team. And while he would later have a career as a policeman, the more modern era recognition of the Dollar name goes to his son. Dr. Creflo A. Dollar is the founder and senior pastor of World Changers Church International (WCCI) in his hometown of College Park, Georgia. The church serves nearly thirty thousand members in New York, Los Angeles, Indianapolis, Washington, D.C., Cleveland, Dallas, Houston and four other Georgia towns. The philosophy of WCCI is: "It is the will of God for you to prosper in every way."

After Creflo Sr. left school, South Fulton won back-to-back titles in 1962 and 1963 for its signature moment in the association.

# Oh Captain, My Captain

Brunswick's first public school for African Americans opened in 1870 as the Freedmen's School. The name was later changed to the Risley School to honor Captain Douglas Gilbert Risley, who had raised funds for the school's construction. In 1936, Risley High School was built and remained in service until 1955, when a new Risley High School was constructed. Both the adjacent Colored Memorial School and Risley High School are landmarks of African American education in Glynn County.

The title the Risley Tigers won in 1957 seemed to be a surprise to everyone who followed GIA football. The Cinderella team traveled to Columbus to take on a Spencer team that had been unbeaten in the 1956 and 1957 seasons—until that game in mid-December. Othller Speakman ran for three scores in the 27–6 win. That was the bookend to Risley's 1950 title, a 40–13 win over Fort Valley–Hunt High. Milton Byard scored three times during that earlier game, with "Choo Choo" Jones and Edward Lowe driving in the other three scores. A former Risley player, Lawrence Coleman, went down in defeat.

Byard claims to have scored fifty touchdowns in that 1950 season, but as with a lot of the individual records at the time, the stats can't be proven.

# The Big Dog

In the city of Atlanta, Washington High was the early GIA champ that ruled Class AA with four titles in the first decade of the organization under legendary coach L.C. Baker. The school won an early pre-GIA title in 1939 over Spencer, and they wouldn't stop there. His Bulldogs only gave up 15 points in 1948, and a reported crowd of ten thousand watched the Class AA game at Herndon Stadium—a 12–0 win over the Atlanta-Howard Ramblers on a rushing score by Big John Andrews and a touchdown pass by Joe Douse.

The city championship was now theirs. The Big Seven Interscholastic Conference championship was theirs. But there was some doubt as to whether they could claim the state title if it was based on the Dickinson System for ranking teams. Washington had lost to Columbus-Radcliff High, but Radcliff had lost to Howard during the regular season as well. Remember what I said about championships and their claims early on? On November 27, 1948, Marion E. Jackson actually wrote in the *Daily World* that

Booker T. Washington High School today.

four teams could stake a claim: Washington, Brooks, Waycross-Center and Savannah–Beach/Cuyler. He followed that statement with: "It only goes to show the disorganization of prep sports in the Deep South."

The Washington High team even went as far as beating Tuskegee Institute's college prep school in a New Year's Day exhibition in the Punch Bowl game to finish their season 10-1.

They went back to back in Class AA in 1949 with a 38–7 win over Laney High of Augusta behind James Bell and Harold Turner. The 1951 title was a 14–6 win over Howard High and gave the blue and white the chance to claim the Big Seven title without needing a playoff.

The website of Booker T. Washington High School boasts to this day, "Our gym is dedicated to Coach L.C. Baker who's [*sic*] football teams had 17 unbeaten seasons and once won 70 straight games. No program in the state of Georgia has come close to matching this." And while that claim would be true, the years of those Bulldog successes are in serious debate— even if you add the twenty other GIA championships the school won in basketball, baseball and track and field in with the football years.

As an aside, the pre-GIA team of 1937 was one of the best of that era. Washington even traveled out of state to play any and all comers—including Baker's brother, who was the head coach of Kentucky-Dunbar. Dunbar and Washington played a continued home-and-home series.

# THE SPENCER LEGACY

Dr. William Henry Spencer was born on September 21, 1857, in Columbus, Georgia. He was a student in the Columbus public school and attended the old Asbury Chapel, and as an adult, he was the principal of the former Fifth Avenue School and the supervisor of the Negro Educational Department. He was dedicated to improving the curriculum of segregated schools and worked to establish courses in the fine arts and vocational education.

African American students in Columbus had to, at times, travel to Atlanta to move beyond a ninth-grade education. Dr. Spencer began working toward opening a high school in Columbus. The idea for such a school was approved, but he passed away on May 30, 1925, five years before the school was built. It was named William Henry Spencer High School in his honor.

Spencer claimed three titles on its own before the GIA existed by 1938, and its successes continued. In 1952, when the so-called Greenies knocked off Atlanta-Howard 12–0 for the 1952 crown, it was widely thought that knocking off all four of the Atlanta schools was an impossible or near impossible feat. But instead, it took Howard until the 1964 title to actually beat Spencer in Columbus. Coach Odis "Big Chief" Spencer did just that, according to the *Atlanta Daily World*, and gave the squad its twenty-first consecutive home win with touchdown runs by quarterback Willie "Babe" Cooper and "Mr. Inside" George Holt.

In 1967, Spencer shut out Risley 25–0 for its last title, which was also its first since 1956. The team had appeared in a title game for the third time in their last four years, but it was also the last game for Spencer in the GIA, as they moved to the GHSA for the 1968 season. The "Big Chief" won his fourth title in twenty years of coaching the green and gold. In an interview with Don Osborn with the *Columbus Ledger*, Spencer (the coach) admitted that the win was the way for Spencer (the school) to leave the GIA: "After the Carver game [the team's only loss in 1967], we dedicated ourselves to winning the state championship. And, along the way, we beat four teams which beat Carver. We feel like we're the best team in the GIA."

In their exit, they tied Washington and Cedar Hill for the most GIA titles—regardless of classification.

In the '70s, the Muscogee County School Board voted to close Spencer High School. The name of the new high school was to be Southwest High School, and its colors were to be blue and white. A group named the Golden Owls appeared in front of both school board and city council meetings to convince them not to eliminate the name of Spencer High School and its green and gold. They were successful.

## WAYCROSS-CENTER HIGH SCHOOL

Center had three titles placed on its mantel before the GIA was through. In 1954, the most powerful team in school history had no problem dispatching Herring High of Decatur 40–0 as the Bulldogs gave up 484 yards on the ground and couldn't get any closer than the 9-yard line on offense. Star running back "Racehorse" William Johnson ran for 209 yards and three scores—32 more yards than Herring had on total offense—and gave Charles Fisher a title as head coach.

Head Coach E.L. Saunders knocked off Perry High for the third title on 1962, riding a wave of desire during which Saunders made sure his players, according to the *Waycross Journal-Herald*, had the "will to win." James Bing, Theodore Johnson and Delano Douglas each scored in the 19–0 shutout. Saunders accepted the championship trophy for his Tigers and admitted that the team was "a great one of which the city would be proud." The players were presented with miniature footballs for their efforts.

## ALL THE TRIVIA YOU NEED
## FOR THE LAST GIA GAME

That honor goes to the Houston Training School and the Tifton-Wilson Tigers in a game that was played on December 5, 1969, in Perry for the Class AA title. It ended in a 14–0 win for Houston. Offensive mistakes (three interceptions, a fumble and a blocked punt) and a tough defensive effort by the Indians kept Wilson off the scoreboard, as they only got as close as the ten-yard line even though they outgained the visitors. Keith Ragin and Larry Green ran in the touchdowns, and Henry Green got credit for the 2-point conversion.

And that was that—almost.

In September 1969, a federal court order from Judge Alexander Lawrence of the Savannah district implemented integrating schools in the state of Georgia under a 6-3-3 plan. The Freedom of Choice plan from the mid-1960s had not been effective in segregating schools to the satisfaction of the courts. A group called the Citizens League for Better Government was trying to encourage ignoring the order altogether, suing a school district in south Georgia to keep it from being implemented period, and tried to orchestrate a boycott of schools that would bring in the 6-3-3 plan. Coffee County schools even closed temporarily for what the *Coffee County Progress* referred to as "to protect life and property" until early October.

Governor Lester Maddox addressed members of the Citizens League in the town of Douglas and said, in defiance of the order, that those people listening to his voice were being denied their rights and that they must not do as the country was doing in Vietnam. They had to fight to win. He wanted them to write President Nixon to express their displeasure as well: "Rather than subject your children to conditions like [those that] exist in Savannah, Atlanta, Washington, and other areas, it would be better to withhold your children from school."

Georgia had ignored the *Brown v. Board of Education* ruling, and Governor Ernest Vandiver even had segregation as one of his platforms when he ran for office in 1960. South Georgia seemed to be going into segregation with the Maddox mindset of "I'd rather fight than switch." But federal funding would be the hammer to make sure integration would happen.

Members of the Citizens League raised money for private schools and eventually opened the Citizens Christian Academy, but segregation was eventually accepted as law. Jack Greenburg wrote in the *Coffee County Progress*: "Altogether school desegregation has been a story of conspicuous achievements, flawed by marked failures...lawyers have their limits, the rest of the job is up to the society."

For the longest time after integration, the Georgia High School Association didn't even recognize the GIA's efforts for champions and championships, but that would change. After Becky Taylor read a series of articles by the *Atlanta Journal-Constitution*'s Derrick Mahone and J.C. Clemons on the GIA in 2002, she expanded on the idea that they brought about: there was a profound lack of organized information on the history of the era. She has since become one of the lead researchers on the GIA in the state over the last decade.

"I saved those articles that they wrote," Taylor admits. "I don't know why. Then I joined a Yahoo! group on the history of Georgia high school football history. It was just a few of us then. I was working with that group doing some research going to the libraries in Valdosta and Tifton. I noticed some GIA scores and thought that they were a little unique."

From there, Taylor assembled a few thousand scores from the history of the football games in the association. She's pretty confident that she has somewhere between 70 and 80 percent of the totals from the schools organized, but she also knows that there are some places where the scores and schools will always have gaps. "Places like Albany and Elberton, I think, will always have holes," Taylor says. "Even as Newnan played a lot of bigger-city teams, those scores may be lost. I know that one school, Forrester, will be hard to find out about in Habersham County in northeast Georgia. They were pretty much a school for the juvenile correctional institute during their time."

Some of her highlights are from places like Boggs Academy (which had to grab kids from wherever it could since it had a student body of only about one hundred as a boarding school) and looking at the history of Cedar Hill High in Cedartown. Taylor also thinks that Escue Rodgers should be in the Georgia Sports Hall of Fame with the records he put in the books with his Cedar Hill Panthers.

Shortly after the *Atlanta Journal-Constitution* articles, the GHSA put the idea of finally recognizing the GIA champs as Georgia state champions to a vote. The vote passed very quickly.

Dr. Ralph Swearngin of the GHSA said about the process:

> As a person who moved to Georgia in 1972, I never experienced the separation of the Georgia Interscholastic Association and the Georgia High School Association. People who held leadership positions in the GHSA in the 1990s told me about their work in the GIA, and there were many wonderful stories about the gifted high school athletes who played in that association. The leadership of the GHSA believed that it was important to recognize the contributions that these players and coaches made to high school athletics in Georgia during the years of segregated education, so all the records we could find from the GIA were archived with the GHSA.

Now, both organizations are looked at under one umbrella for their champs. But the information of the GIA is still coming to light after all the years of discovery, recognition and acceptance.

Chapter 9

# THE FUTURE OF GEORGIA FOOTBALL

The largest issue confronting high school football in the state of Georgia as we all move forward is what a lot of activities and businesses see these days: growth and economics. The 2010 United States Census registered a growth rate of 18.3 percent for the state of Georgia with the fourth-highest amount of population change at just over 1.5 million people. The Atlanta metropolitan area grew by almost a full quarter from 2000 to 2010, accounted for almost half of the state's entire population and holds almost two-thirds of the state's growth on the whole in the last ten years. Three Georgia counties—Forsyth, Paulding and Henry—are in the top ten in the entire United States for population explosions.

All this means that Georgia school systems had to expand to meet the student demands. The GHSA says that there are now 443 member schools as opposed to the 20 percent less of a number that was around in 1990. The GHSA was faced with the idea of reorganizing for the first time in a little over a decade, and the association weighed its options to figure out a solution. The suggestions were: going from pre-2000 levels of four classifications to expanding to six classifications like some neighboring states; or, in the end, not doing anything and staying at the number five. Part of the idea of retraction had a twist. There would be four classes but north and south champions—much like the days when the GHSA didn't exist and the governing body was in its infancy.

In mid-May 2011, the decision was made by a 26–24 vote that Georgia would expand into six classifications like its neighbor, Alabama. That plan received the majority vote needed from the 50 executive committee members, and it will go into effect for the 2012–13 school year. Had the current five-classification format stayed, it would have remained in place through the 2013–14 school year.

"It's going to be a significant change," Georgia High School Association executive director Dr. Ralph Swearngin admitted to Mark Harmon in an interview for Georgia Public Broadcasting's *SportsCentral XL* program. "We haven't added a classification since 2000 and, at our meeting of the Executive Committee, it was decided that we would go from five classifications to six. We won't know where schools are placed until the enrollment numbers are known in October of 2011."

The opinions around the state were from every direction possible when the vote was approved—positive, negative and all points in between. Dr. Swearngin asked for more of a prudent approach and waiting for every possible variable to pan out before rendering any kind of final judgment. He admitted:

> *They've read some media accounts…some of the worksheet information if we had gone to six classifications two-and-a-half years ago…we really won't know anything until then.*
>
> *It's been an interesting few months because we really haven't come to develop any strong consensus. The original plan that was voted out of the Executive Committee was to have four classifications and split the eight championships. That was pretty soundly defeated 35 to 15. And, then, the second topic that was discussed these past few months was the straight six classifications. 26–24 is hardly a mandate, but that's the way we're going.*
>
> *I think the bottom line was that everyone was looking for some way* [that] *schools of similar size could play closer to home for their regular season and then they would have championships for schools that were strictly of similar size. There were some questions about a radical change. The fix was a change, but it wasn't quite as radical. I think that was the reason we decided to go that way.*

But remember, it was only one vote that kept the reclassification from happening at all on that second round of the voting process. If it had been 25–25, everything that Georgia knew as its sports landscape would still be in place.

"Five classifications was the default position," Swearngin says. "We're really going to have to make some adjustments for our playoffs—especially our championships. It won't impact how we televise certain things. Some championships are easy—one more championship in football? That's easy."

The debate for just how many classifications the state will have is debated on two-year cycles. The constitution and bylaws have it written that the Reclassification Committee can propose any number of classifications and/ or regions dividing the four-hundred-plus schools in the 159 counties across the state. There was even a debate in years past to see if the reclassification debate could come up every four years instead of the current two-year setup.

"But that's like getting a root canal every four years instead of every two years," Swearngin says, laughing. "The state is changing so rapidly that the population demographics are such that we can't wait every four years to make changes."

The Department of Education attendance numbers for every member school in the GHSA that are released in the fall won't have an impact on the schools that will now inhabit each of the six classes. It will be determined by percentage. The top 15 percent, or sixty-six schools, will be in the new AAAAAA class. There will be 21 percent of the member schools in the new AAAAA, and the remaining 64 percent will be evenly divided among the lower four classes. The procedures for membership, attendance and population being part of the GHSA haven't changed in this process.

Schools should have the option to "play up" if they petition the GHSA and ask for that adjustment—regardless of the number of students who attend classes on a given campus. Savannah schools, as an example, are more suited to be in AA because of their numbers but play in AAAAA because of geography and budget concerns. And those will always be concerns for schools in the current economic environment. Schools will also have the opportunity to appeal their new status because of projected enrollment figures and could move up or down in class. That's another wrinkle in this entire proceeding—especially when there are seventy-two thousand athletes participating in spring sports alone.

On the field, changes took place all over, starting in Thomson with the retirement of Luther Welsh. Coach Welsh conquered lymphoma in the past decade but succumbed to the disease in July 2011. Both he and his wife, Anne, were facing battles with the disease and, at the end of the 2010 season, decided that it was time for him to return home to Bishopville, South Carolina, and leave the coaching to another.

Anne had half of a lung removed in September 2010 as part of her battle, Coach Welsh traveled to Augusta for his own treatments for esophageal cancer. The couple, who will have been married fifty years in September, was looking to enjoy their time at home. "The devil is trying to get us," Anne told the *Augusta Chronicle*'s Scott Michaux after she fell and broke her hip during her own recovery in 2010.

The new Bulldogs coach comes from the town of Twin City, otherwise known as Greymont-Summit. Milan Turner won a Class A title at ECI with Georgia tailback Washaun Ealey in 2007, and he understands his new place—having been chosen over one hundred other applicants.

"You don't replace a Coach Welsh," Turner said after his unanimous confirmation by the McDuffie County School Board in February. "He leaves a legacy that will stand. It's a great honor to follow a coaching legend like Luther Welsh. I understand the expectations. I understand the tradition."

Welsh passes on having coached his way into the top eight on the all-time national list of most games coached. Welsh coached 507 games with eleven different schools, winning 329 of them. His record at Thomson was 174-47-2 with the Bulldogs, and his overall record was 333-181-6.

Steve Pardue, after a lot of years being courted by the University of Kentucky, is finally moving to Lexington to coach the running backs under Joker Phillips. The kid who grew up in Hopkinsville, Kentucky, is heading home.

"I've watched Steve for a lot of years and how he handles himself as a coach," Phillips told Chip Cosby of the *Lexington Herald-Leader* in January 2011. "He's earned the respect of his players and of his fellow coaches through his work on the state boards in Georgia. Being a Kentucky native, he brings a lot to the table in Kentucky and Georgia." That—and the seemingly endless pipeline of players who went from LaGrange to Lexington.

"The number one reason I came to Kentucky is because of Joker Phillips," Pardue told Cosby. "I believe in the way he's doing things here and his vision for the program. And, because it's the University of Kentucky, the state school of my home state. This was the toughest decision I've ever made, to leave the town of LaGrange, and if it weren't for Joker Phillips and the University of Kentucky, I wouldn't have left. But I'm ready for a new challenge and am excited about the future of Kentucky football."

Lee Campbell, who won titles at Hawkinsville in 2003 and 2004, moved on to the town of Cordele and Crisp County High. "I'm very excited about the new opportunity," Campbell told Jonathan Heeter of the *Macon Telegraph* in March 2011. "The community has been great. The facilities are great. There's a lot of potential at Crisp County." Campbell left after three seasons in Eastman, at Dodge County High, where his teams went 10-20. "We didn't do as well as I would have liked for sure," Campbell said.

The Cougars advanced to the semifinals at the Georgia Dome in 1995. They haven't had back-to-back winning seasons since the 1995–97 seasons.

In April 2011, the Lincoln County community lost Thomas Bunch at the age of ninety. "He meant all the world," Campbell told the *Augusta Chronicle*. "I don't know if there's a finer person that I ever met." There was a visitation at the new Lincoln County High School on the west side of town—complete with his trophies—before the services at the Lincolnton Baptist Church.

"He was a Christian through and through," said Campbell, who served as a pallbearer at Bunch's funeral. "He was a great father and community person. I don't see how anybody could find anything negative to say. I can't say enough good things about him. I was fortunate to be considered one of his adopted children."

Rance Gillespie is only 189 wins away from a special place in the hearts of Wildcats fans—thanks to a promise from David Waller. When Gillespie accepted the job at Valdosta High School, Waller took the new coach for a ride in his pickup truck. When asked about clarifying the story, Gillespie doesn't even need to know what you're going to ask him about: "It's true," he says almost immediately.

Could Rance Gillespie's efforts in Valdosta take up a lot of room in here at the Valdosta Wildcats Museum?

"I just wanted to take him around town to introduce him to some people I thought he ought to know—the Boys and Girls Club, the people at my church, businesspeople," Waller says. "But I said that we were going to Sunset Hill Cemetery first. They can hear all the shouting on Friday night, you know."

Gillespie says:

> When I first got the job, he asked me if he could pick me up because he thought there were some people that he wanted me to meet. We drove directly to the graveyard. I was wondering, but as we drove in he started giving me a history lesson, which is cool. And being coach here, I think it's very important. He was telling me about the different coaches that were buried there. We got out and we were walking down a row of plots, and he said this was where Coach Bazemore is buried and here was where Coach Hyder was buried.

"They sit out here on Friday night, and they can hear the game, you know," Waller told him. "They know whether it's a bad call from the officials because they can hear all the booing or whether it's a touchdown. Coach Buck Thomas, who was coach during World War II while Coach Bazemore was in the navy, Coach Bazemore and Coach Hyder won 518 games among them. I said I've got six more plots right here."

Gillespie continues:

> David said that this is where he planned to be buried. Coach Bazemore is buried at the far right of that row. And then there's a couple of places, and then there's David's. Then there's where Coach Hyder is. He said, "Now, I own that spot right there also. And if you win 200 ballgames, I'll fit you right there."
>
> I said, "Yes, sir, absolutely." It just signifies the importance of football here. Mr. Waller is such an asset to the football program and to the community. He's done so many good things for Valdosta. It's unbelievable.

Gillespie is embracing the expectations as the winningest high school football program in the country and is looking forward to getting the team where it once was, since you can go anywhere around the world and be asked how the Wildcats are doing.

Or here? The new granite and brick display on the outside wall.

Waller says with conviction:

> *Coach Bazemore and Coach Hyder built what we are today. We're winners.*
> *We are Titletown. If anybody disputes that, come by with a better claim.*
> *We believe that. We believe we're Winnersville, and we have the record to*
> *prove it. If everybody in your community believes that, then that's what you*
> *are. We're different. We want to win. We're willing to pay the price to win.*
> *And we're going to be winners. It's because of those two men and those two*
> *different groups of people—and you've got to put that into perspective—*
> *they were willing to pay the price and do whatever it took in the trenches.*
> *You can't put it in dollars. You can only put it in history.*

And, as happens as every new football season comes in front of all of us, optimism and a new sense of history—the history in place and the history that is to happen as we all watch—visit us once more.

| Year | AAAAA | AAAA | AAA |
|------|-------|------|-----|
| 1947 | | | |
| 1948 | | | |
| 1949 | | | |
| 1950 | | | |
| 1951 | | | |
| 1952 | | | |
| 1953 | | | |
| 1954 | | | |
| 1955 | | | |
| 1956 | | | Richmond Academy |
| 1957 | | | Northside, Atlanta |
| 1958 | | | LaGrange |
| 1959 | | | Albany |
| 1960 | | | Valdosta |
| 1961 | | | Valdosta |
| 1962 | | | Valdosta |
| 1963 | | | Avondale |
| 1964 | | | Glynn Academy |

# Appendix A

# GHSA Champions

| AA | A | B | C |
|---|---|---|---|
| Lanier | | | |
| Lanier | Fitzgerald | West Point | Fort Valley |
| Brown | Decatur | Adel | Quitman |
| Decatur | Rockmart | West Point | Quitman |
| Richmond Academy | Valdosta | Cordele | Forest Park |
| Murphy | Valdosta | Hogansville | Calhoun |
| Grady | Valdosta | Model | Hawkinsville |
| Rossville | Jesup | Model | Hawkinsville |
| Rossville/ LaGrange (tie) | Athens | Morgan County | Monticello |
| Valdosta | Carrollton/ Statesboro (tie) | Morgan County | Monticello |
| Valdosta | Statesboro | Trion | Waynesboro |
| Avondale/ Thomasville (tie) | Stephens County | Morgan County | West Point |
| Wayne County | Dublin | Morgan County | Hawkinsville |
| Waycross | Dublin | Washington-Wilkes | Lincolnton |
| Waycross | Carrollton | Fort Valley | Coosa |
| Rossville | Americus | Morgan County | Lincolnton |
| Cedartown | Dublin | Washington-Wilkes | Lincolnton |
| Douglas County | Carrollton | Blakely | Davis |

| Year | AAAAA | AAAA | AAA |
|------|-------|------|-----|
| 1965 | | | Valdosta |
| 1966 | | | Valdosta |
| 1967 | | | Marietta |
| 1968 | | | Valdosta |
| 1969 | | | Athens/ Valdosta (tie) |
| 1970 | | | Lakeside |
| 1971 | | | Valdosta |
| 1972 | | | Lakeside |
| 1973 | | | Thomasville |
| 1974 | | | Thomasville |
| 1975 | | | Central, Macon |
| 1976 | | | Warner Robins |
| 1977 | | | Clarke Central |
| 1978 | | Griffin/ Valdosta (tie) | Westminster |
| 1979 | | Clarke Central | Redan |
| 1980 | | Lowndes | Woodward Academy |
| 1981 | | Warner Robins | Waycross |
| 1982 | | Valdosta | Bainbridge |
| 1983 | | Tift County | Mitchell-Baker |
| 1984 | | Valdosta | Thomson |
| 1985 | | Clarke Central | Thomson |
| 1986 | | Valdosta | Villa Rica |
| 1987 | | Morrow | Worth County |
| 1988 | | Warner Robins | Thomasville |

# GHSA Champions

| AA | A | B | C |
|---|---|---|---|
| West Rome | Americus | Bradwell Institute | Warren County |
| North Fulton | Statesboro | Washington-Wilkes | Warren County |
| Dalton | Thomson | Washington-Wilkes | Putnam County |
| St. Pius X | Thomson | Roswell | Warren County |
| North Springs | Coosa | Vidalia | Savannah Country Day |
| Woodward Academy | Roswell | Lovett | Mt. de Sales |
| Westminster | Carrollton | Bowdon | Mt. de Sales |
| Southwest DeKalb | Carrollton | Southeast Bulloch | |
| Southwest Atlanta | Mt. de Sales | Southeast Bulloch | |
| Americus | Carrollton | Trion | |
| Americus | Irwin County | Lyons | |
| Avondale | Turner County | Lincoln County | |
| Waycross | East Rome | Lincoln County | |
| East Rome | Buford | | |
| Model | Johnson County | | |
| Mary Persons | Greenville | | |
| Commerce | Douglass, Montezuma | | |
| West Rome | Palmetto | | |
| West Rome | Palmetto | | |
| West Rome | Greenville | | |
| West Rome | Lincoln County | | |
| Central, Carrollton | Lincoln County | | |
| Central, Carrollton | Lincoln County | | |
| R.E. Lee | Clinch County | | |

| Year | AAAAA | AAAA | AAA |
|------|-------|------|-----|
| 1989 | | Valdosta | Marist |
| 1990 | | Valdosta | Cairo |
| 1991 | | LaGrange | Kendrick/ Lakeside, DeKalb (tie) |
| 1992 | | Valdosta | Thomas County Central |
| 1993 | | Dunwoody | Thomas County Central |
| 1994 | | Colquitt County | Thomas County Central |
| 1995 | | Southwest DeKalb | Josey |
| 1996 | | Brookwood | Thomas County Central |
| 1997 | | Parkview | Thomas County Central |
| 1998 | | Valdosta | Dougherty |
| 1999 | | Lowndes | Oconee County |
| 2000 | Parkview | Shaw | Swainsboro |
| 2001 | Parkview | Statesboro | LaGrange |
| 2002 | Parkview | Thomson | Screven County |
| 2003 | Camden County | Marist | LaGrange |
| 2004 | Lowndes | Warner Robins | LaGrange |
| 2005 | Lowndes | Statesboro | Peach County |
| 2006 | Peachtree Ridge/ Roswell (tie) | Northside, Warner Robins | Peach County |
| 2007 | Lowndes | Northside, Warner Robins | Carver, Columbus |
| 2008 | Camden County | Tucker | Cairo |
| 2009 | Camden County | Sandy Creek | Peach County |
| 2010 | Brookwood | Chattahoochee | Sandy Creek |

# GHSA Champions

| AA | A | B | C |
|---|---|---|---|
| Mitchell-Baker | Lincoln County | | |
| Pepperell | Lincoln County | | |
| Cartersville | Clinch County | | |
| Mitchell-Baker | Bowdon | | |
| Greene-Taliaferro | Lincoln County | | |
| Washington County | Brooks County | | |
| Elbert County | Lincoln County | | |
| Washington County | Macon County | | |
| Washington County | Manchester | | |
| Carrollton | Darlington | | |
| Cartersville | Charlton County | | |
| Americus | Commerce | | |
| Americus | Buford | | |
| Buford | Clinch County | | |
| Buford | Hawkinsville | | |
| Charlton County | Hawkinsville/ Clinch County (tie) | | |
| Charlton County | Lincoln County | | |
| Charlton County/ Dublin (tie) | Lincoln County | | |
| Buford | Emanuel County Institute | | |
| Buford | Wesleyan | | |
| Buford | Wilcox County | | |
| Buford | Clinch County | | |

# Appendix B

# DALTON HIGH SCHOOL WIN STREAK

## *FIFTY-ONE YEARS CONSECUTIVE WITH WINNING RECORD*

| 1960 | 5-4-1 | |
| 1961 | 8-2 | |
| 1962 | 9-1 | |
| 1963 | 9-2 | |
| 1964 | 11-2 | AA State Runner-up |
| 1965 | 8-3 | Sub-Region Champion |
| 1966 | 9-2-2 | AA State Runner-up |
| 1967 | 12-1 | AA State Champion |
| 1968 | 10-2 | AAA State Semifinalist |
| 1969 | 7-2-1 | |
| 1970 | 11-1 | AAA State Semifinalist |
| 1971 | 8-2 | |
| 1972 | 6-3-1 | |
| 1973 | 6-4 | |
| 1974 | 5-4-1 | |
| 1975 | 9-5 | AA State Runner-up |
| 1976 | 10-2 | AA State Semifinalist |
| 1977 | 12-2 | AAA State Runner-up |
| 1978 | 13-2 | AAA State Runner-up |

# Dalton High School Win Streak

| 1979 | 10-4 | AAA State Semifinalist |
|------|------|------------------------|
| 1980 | 10-1 | Sub-Region Champion |
| 1981 | 12-1 | AAA State Quarterfinalist |
| 1982 | 12-2 | AAA State Semifinalist |
| 1983 | 6-4 | |
| 1984 | 7-3-1 | Region Playoffs |
| 1985 | 11-1 | Sub-Region Champion |
| 1986 | 11-1 | Sub-Region Champion |
| 1987 | 9-2-1 | Sub-Region Champion |
| 1988 | 13-1 | AAA State Semifinalist |
| 1989 | 7-4 | Region Champion |
| 1990 | 9-1-2 | Region Co-Champion |
| 1991 | 9-2 | Sub-Region Champion |
| 1992 | 11-2 | AAA State Quarterfinalist |
| 1993 | 12-1 | AAA State Semifinalist |
| 1994 | 13-1 | AAA State Semifinalist |
| 1995 | 8-3 | Region Playoffs |
| 1996 | 10-3 | AAA State Quarterfinalist |
| 1997 | 8-3 | Region Champion |
| 1998 | 10-3 | AAA State Quarterfinalist |
| 1999 | 6-5 | AAA State Playoffs |
| 2000 | 7-4 | AAAA State Playoffs |
| 2001 | 13-2 | AAAA State Runner-up |
| 2002 | 8-2 | |
| 2003 | 8-2 | |
| 2004 | 6-4 | |
| 2005 | 10-3 | AAAA State Quarterfinalist |
| 2006 | 9-2 | AAA State Playoffs |
| 2007 | 9-2 | Region Champions |
| 2008 | 7-3 | |
| 2009 | 7-4 | AAA State Playoffs |
| 2010 | 7-3 | |

# Appendix C

# Larry Campbell's Coaching Record

## Lincoln County High School

| 1972 | 3-7 | |
|------|-----|---|
| 1973 | 8-1-1 | Region Champs |
| 1974 | 9-4 | South Georgia Champs |
| 1975 | 9-3 | Sectional Champs |
| 1976 | 13-0 | State Champs |
| 1977 | 13-0 | State Champs |
| 1978 | 12-1 | Region Champs |
| 1979 | 14-1 | South Georgia Champs |
| 1980 | 9-3 | Region Runner-up |
| 1981 | 9-2 | Third in region |
| 1982 | 12-1 | Sectional Champs |
| 1983 | 12-2 | Sectional Champs |
| 1984 | 12-2-1 | South Georgia Champs |
| 1985 | 15-0 | State Champs |
| 1986 | 13-2 | State Champs |
| 1987 | 15-0 | State Champs |
| 1988 | 10-3 | Region Champs |
| 1989 | 15-0 | State Champs |

# Larry Campbell's Coaching Record

| 1990 | 15-0  | State Champs         |
|------|-------|----------------------|
| 1991 | 14-1  | State Runner-up      |
| 1992 | 11-2  | First-Round Winner   |
| 1993 | 15-0  | State Champs         |
| 1994 | 8-3-1 | Region Champs        |
| 1995 | 15-0  | State Champs         |
| 1996 | 9-2   | Region Champs        |
| 1997 | 13-1  | State Quarterfinals  |
| 1998 | 13-2  | State Runner-up      |
| 1999 | 11-4  | State Runner-up      |
| 2000 | 10-4  | State Quarterfinals  |
| 2001 | 6-6   | First-Round Winner   |
| 2002 | 8-5   | Second-Round Winner  |
| 2003 | 14-1  | State Runner-up      |
| 2004 | 12-2  | State Quarterfinals  |
| 2005 | 12-3  | State Champs         |
| 2006 | 14-1  | State Champs         |
| 2007 | 11-2  | State Quarterfinals  |
| 2008 | 12-2  | State Semifinals     |
| 2009 | 11-2  | State Quarterfinals  |
| 2010 | 10-3  | State Quarterfinals  |

Totals    447-78-3 (.849)
Youngest Coach to Win 300 Games, Twenty-fifth Nationally
Currently Seventh in United States in Career Wins

As of November 2010, John McKissick had completed his fifty-ninth season at Summerville High School (South Carolina) with a record of 586-138-13.

# Appendix D

# THE LONGEST WINNING STREAK

## *BUFORD HIGH SCHOOL*

### 2001 (15-0) State Champs

| August 24 | Decatur | Won 41–21 |
|---|---|---|
| August 31 | Central, Carroll | Won 30–18 |
| September 7 | Loganville | Won 44–0 |
| September 21 | Central Gwinnett | Won 42–21 |
| September 28 | Bowdon | Won 40–0 |
| October 5 | Lincoln County | Won 31–6 |
| October 26 | Jefferson | Won 41–0 |
| November 2 | Wesleyan | Won 27–0 |
| November 9 | Commerce | Won 41–0 |
| November 16 | Trion | Won 40–0 |
| November 23 | Social Circle | Won 49–12 |
| November 30 | Mt. Zion, Carroll | Won 58–22 |
| December 7 | Johnson County | Won 21–6 |
| December 14 | Clinch County | Won 15–7 |
| December 22 | Bowdon | Won 35–13 |

# The Longest Winning Streak

## 2002 (15-0) State Champs

| September 6 | Central, Carroll | Won 50–7 |
|---|---|---|
| September 20 | Rabun County | Won 31–6 |
| September 27 | Banks County | Won 42–0 |
| October 4 | Greater Atlanta Christian | Won 35–10 |
| October 11 | Lumpkin County | Won 35–3 |
| October 18 | Union County | Won 49–6 |
| October 25 | Wesleyan | Won 49–13 |
| November 1 | Madison County | Won 21–7 |
| November 8 | Apalachee | Won 28–0 |
| November 15 | Dawson County | Won 47–9 |
| November 22 | Decatur | Won 41–0 |
| November 29 | Putnam County | Won 34–0 |
| December 6 | Pierce County | Won 35–26 |
| December 13 | Americus | Won 38–12 |
| December 20 | Greater Atlanta Christian | Won 34–10 |

## 2003 (15-0) State Champs

| September 5 | Central, Carroll | Won 45–0 |
|---|---|---|
| September 19 | Rabun County | Won 52–0 |
| September 26 | Banks County | Won 38–0 |
| October 3 | Greater Atlanta Christian | Won 30–0 |
| October 10 | Lumpkin County | Won 20–9 |
| October 17 | Union County | Won 49–10 |
| October 24 | Wesleyan | Won 43–3 |
| October 31 | Madison County | Won 41–8 |
| November 7 | Apalachee | Won 49–0 |
| November 14 | Dawson County | Won 46–7 |
| November 21 | Blessed Trinity | Won 56–6 |
| November 28 | Adairsville | Won 48–19 |
| December 5 | Cook | Won 30–12 |
| December 13 | Decatur | Won 42–13 |
| December 20 | Charlton County | Won 31–3 |

## 2004 (13-2) State Runner-Up

| August 27 | Lumpkin County | Won 41–7 |
| September 3 | Union County | Won 49–0 |
| September 10 | Central Gwinnett | Lost 20–14 |
| September 17 | Gainesville | Won 31–14 |
| September 24 | East Hall | Won 48–14 |
| October 1 | Dawson County | Won 45–10 |
| October 8 | Wesleyan | Won 35–0 |
| October 15 | Banks County | Won 45–0 |
| October 22 | Greater Atlanta Christian | Won 31–28 |
| October 29 | Rabun County | Won 31–0 |
| November 5 | Chattooga | Won 34–14 |
| November 12 | Morgan County | Won 38–7 |
| November 19 | Brooks County | Won 36–21 |
| November 27 | Dublin | Won 28–24 |
| December 4 | Charlton County | Lost 35–20 |

# Appendix E

# TEAM AND PLAYER STATISTICS

Passing Yards (Career)—minimum 5000

| YARDS | PLAYER | SCHOOL | YEARS |
|---|---|---|---|
| 9062 | Zach Stanford | Metter | 2001–4 |
| 8427 | Drew Little | Henry County | 2005–8 |
| 8281 | Fabian Walker | Americus | 1996–98 |
| 8265 | Hutson Mason | Lassiter | 2007–9 |
| 8226 | Cedric Johnson | Americus | 2001–4 |
| 7655 | Dwight Dasher | Charlton County | 2003–6 |
| 7568 | Caleb Horvath | Chattahoochee County | 2006–8 |
| 7487 | Jeremy Privett | Charlton County | 2000–3 |
| 7147 | Brent Owens | Dooly County | 1998–2001 |
| 6616 | Al Pinkins | Mitchell-Baker | 1988–90 |
| 6496 | Mikey Tamburo | North Gwinnett | 2006–8 |
| 6062 | Jonathan Carkhuff | Lovett | 2007–9 |
| 5965 | Kurtis Koester | Cherokee | 1998–2001 |
| 5749 | Dre Prather | Gordon Central | 2008–10 |
| 5607 | Brad Schlosser | North Gwinnett | 2004–5 |
| 5505 | Barrett Wilkes | Lowndes | 2001 |
| 5500 | Bo Hatchett | Habersham Central | 2004–7 |
| 5497 | Todd Coley | Hawkinsville | 2002–4 |
| 5486 | Jack Rackley | Westwood School & Mitchell-Baker | 1989–92 |

| YARDS | PLAYER | SCHOOL | YEARS |
|---|---|---|---|
| 5214 | Buck Belue | Valdosta | 1974–77 |
| 5210 | Eric Jackson | Turner County | 1993–96 |
| 5192 | A.J. Bryant | Peach County | 2001–3 |
| 5167 | Mike Bobo | Thomasville | 1989–92 |
| 5111 | Todd Wells | Forest Park | 1993–95 |
| 5029 | David Greene | South Gwinnett | 1997–99 |

Points Allowed (Season)—maximum 10

| POINTS | SCHOOL | YEAR |
|---|---|---|
| 0 | Lincolnton | 1930 (7 games) |
| 2 | Boys' High | 1940 |
| 6 | Albany | 1927 |
| 6 | Valdosta | 1938 |
| 8 | Thomasville | 1928 |
| 8 | Americus | 1975 |
| 10 | Valdosta | 1924 |
| 10 | Manchester | 1984 |

Receiving Yards (Career)—minimum 3000

| YARDS | PLAYER | SCHOOL | YEARS |
|---|---|---|---|
| 4477 | Stan Rome | Valdosta | 1971–73 |
| 4343 | Jermaine Allen | Americus | 2000–3 |
| 4002 | Blake Gowder | Union County | 2006–9 |
| 3396 | Niko Jones | Chattahoochee County | 2007–9 |
| 3395 | Chris Slaughter | Peach County | 2003–5 |
| 3270 | Tavarres King | Habersham Central | 2004–7 |
| 3197 | Andre Hastings | Morrow | 1987–89 |
| 3182 | Justin Williams | Charlton County | 2002–5 |

# Team and Player Statistics

Rushing Yards (Career)—minimum 6000

| YARDS | PLAYER | SCHOOL | YEARS |
|---|---|---|---|
| 8844 | Monte Williams | Commerce | 1997–2000 |
| 7841 | Robert Toomer | Worth County | 1988–91 |
| 7695 | Chris Clay | Randolph-Clay | 2004–7 |
| 7322 | Eddie Dixon | ECI | 1980–83 |
| 6923 | Brett Millican | Parkview | 1992–95 |
| 6920 | Greg Williams | Metter | 1980–83 |
| 6429 | Micah Andrews | GAC | 1999–2002 |
| 6385 | Charles Grant | Miller County | 1994–97 |
| 6374 | Don Calloway | Miller County | 1996–99 |
| 6349 | Audell Grace | Screven County | 1991–94 |
| 6338 | Darius Marshall | Baldwin | 2003–6 |
| 6279 | Travis Evans | Westside Macon | 2000–3 |
| 6155 | Chris Cole | Brooks County | 1991–94 |
| 6137 | Herschel Walker | Johnson County | 1976–79 |

Team Scoring (Season)—minimum 600

| POINTS | SCHOOL | YEAR |
|---|---|---|
| 682 | Dublin | 2006 |
| 681 | Buford | 2007 |
| 644 | Miller County | 1997 |
| 642 | Camden County | 2008 |
| 639 | Fitzgerald | 2009 |
| 636 | Calhoun | 2005 |
| 635 | Carrollton | 2010 |
| 630 | Washington County | 1994 |
| 629 | Valdosta | 1971 |
| 629 | Gainesville | 2009 |

| POINTS | SCHOOL | YEAR |
|---|---|---|
| 628 | Clinch County | 2010 |
| 625 | Northside (Warner Robins) | 1999 |
| 616 | Emanuel County Institute | 2007 |
| 614 | Warner Robins | 1976 |
| 612 | Southeast Bulloch | 1972 |
| 611 | Dublin | 2005 |
| 609 | Thomson | 2002 |
| 607 | Tucker | 2010 |

Shutouts (Season)—minimum 10

| SHUTOUTS | TEAM | YEAR |
|---|---|---|
| 13 | Americus | 1975 |
| 11 | Valdosta | 1969 |
| 11 | West Rome | 1985 |
| 10 | Moultrie | 1937 |
| 10 | Washington | 1940 |
| 10 | Boys' High | 1943 |
| 10 | Fort Valley | 1957 |
| 10 | North Fulton | 1960 |
| 10 | Lincolnton | 1963 |
| 10 | Thomson | 1967 |
| 10 | Douglass (Montezuma) | 1981 |
| 10 | Manchester | 1984 |
| 10 | Turner County | 1971 |

Touchdown Passes (Career)—minimum 60

| TDs | PLAYER | SCHOOL | YEARS |
|---|---|---|---|
| 92 | Jeremy Privett | Charlton County | 2000–3 |
| 92 | Cedric Johnson | Americus | 2001–4 |

# Team and Player Statistics

| TDs | PLAYER | SCHOOL | YEARS |
|-----|--------|--------|-------|
| 87 | Dwight Dasher | Charlton County | 2003–6 |
| 85 | Hutson Mason | Lassiter | 2007–9 |
| 81 | Fabian Walker | Americus | 1996–98 |
| 80 | Brent Owens | Dooly County | 1998–2001 |
| 80 | Drew Little | Henry County | 2005–8 |
| 72 | Jake Rackley | Westwood School and Mitchell-Baker | 1989–92 |
| 72 | Caleb Horvath | Chattahoochee County | 2006–8 |
| 67 | Al Pinkins | Mitchell-Baker | 1988–90 |
| 66 | Todd Coley | Hawkinsville | 2002–4 |
| 62 | Rodney Hudson | LaGrange | 1988–91 |
| 60 | Dion Graham | Thomasville | 1996–98 |
| 60 | Brad Lunsford | Jackson | 2004–6 |

Touchdowns (Game)—minimum 7

| TDs | PLAYER | SCHOOL | V. | DATE |
|-----|--------|--------|-----|------|
| 10 | Kenneth Moore | Calhoun | Acworth | 10-15-48 (he added 2 PAT for 62 points) |
| 8 | Don Calloway | Miller Co. | Lanier Co. | 9-3-99 |
| 8 | Thomas Flowers | Pebblebrook | East Paulding | 2001 |
| 7 | Arlie New | Washington-Wilkes | Waynesboro | 1921 |
| 7 | Larry Hooks | McNair | Druid Hills | 9-1-90 |
| 7 | Selma Calloway | Miller Co. | Dale Co., AL | 10-9-92 |
| 7 | Leon White | Norcross | South Gwinnett | 10-28-95 |
| 7 | Courtnee Slaughter | Eagles Landing | Salem | 10-10-96 |
| 7 | Chucky Marks | Monroe, Alb. | Leon, FL | 9-12-97 |
| 7 | Daccus Turman | Washington-Wilkes | Commerce | 2000 |
| 7 | Cameron Smith | Brookwood | Meadowcreek | 2005 |

| TDs | PLAYER | SCHOOL | v. | DATE |
|---|---|---|---|---|
| 7 | Kendrick Harris | Gainesville | Pickens | 2007 |
| 7 | Washaun Ealey | ECI | Calvary Day | 2007 |
| 7 | Toney Williams | Milton | Chattahoochee | 2008 |
| 7 | Darrien Hudson | Eagles Landing Christian Academy | Warren County | 2009 |
| 7 | Carter Haley | North Whitfield | Valley Point | 1962 |

Touchdowns (Career)—minimum 70

| TDs | PLAYER | SCHOOL | YEARS |
|---|---|---|---|
| 133 | Washaun Ealey | ECI | 2006–9 |
| 111 | Matt Dunham | Pacelli | 2001–4 |
| 105 | Robert Toomer | Worth County | 1988–91 |
| 105 | Monte Williams | Commerce | 1997–2000 |
| 101 | Charles Grant | Miller County | 1995–97 |
| 91 | Darius Walker | Buford | 2000–3 |
| 89 | Chris Clay | Randolph-Clay | 2004–7 |
| 86 | Herschel Walker | Johnson County | 1977–79 |
| 81 | Debrale Smiley | Thomas County Central | 2004–7 |
| 76 | Roddy Jones | Chamblee | 2004–6 |
| 74 | Travis Evans | Westside Macon | 2000–3 |
| 74 | Darius Marshall | Baldwin | 2003–6 |
| 72 | Runt Moon | Commerce | 1970–73 |
| 72 | Jeremy Marshall | Hawkinsville | 2002–5 |
| 71 | Garrison Hearst | Lincoln County | 1986–89 |
| 70 | Melvin Borum | Hawkinsville | 1951–54 |
| 70 | Chris Cole | Brooks County | 1991–94 |

Courtesy: Georgia High School Football Historical Association- ghsfha.org

# Appendix F
# CAREER COACHING WINS

| COACH | SCHOOL | RECORD |
|-------|--------|--------|
| Larry Campbell | Lincoln County | 447-78-3 |
| Robert Davis | retired, 2009 | 355-73-1 |
| Dan Pitts | retired, 1997 | 346-109-4 |
| Luther Welsh | retired, 2010 | 324-137-6 |
| T. McFerrin | Jefferson | 318-98-4 |
| Bill Chappell | retired, 1996 | 317-74-9 |
| Wayman Creel | deceased, 1990 | 315-105-2 |
| Dwight Hochstetler | Bowdon | 309-103-1 |
| Nick Hyder | deceased, 1996 | 302-48-5 |
| Robert Herring | retired, 2009 | 301-118-3 |
| Rodney Walker | Mary Persons | 291-138-3 |
| Alan Chadwick | Marist | 290-51 |
| Billy Henderson | retired, 1996 | 286-107-15 |
| Robbie Pruitt | Fitzgerald | 283-53 |
| Graham Hixon | deceased, 2005 | 279-91-17 |
| John Hill | retired, 2000 | 270-89-3 |
| Charles Winslette | Greene Co. | 269-122-4 |
| Wright Bazemore | deceased | 268-51-7 |
| Charlie Grisham | deceased | 261-69-13 |
| Buck Godfrey | SW DeKalb | 258-82 |

| Coach | School | Record |
|---|---|---|
| Dexter Wood | retired, 2004 | 257-92-3 |
| Jim Lofton | retired, 1998 | 255-112-3 |
| Bobby Gruhn | deceased | 255-103-5 |
| Robert Akins | Ringgold | 249-147 |
| Jim Cavan | deceased, 1983 | 248-120-23 |
| Ray Lamb | retired, 1992 | 248-104-11 |
| Jim Hughes | retired, 1999 | 247-102-5 |
| Charlie Davidson | retired, 1984 | 244-96-14 |
| Tommy Stringer | retired | 242-174-6 |
| Conrad Nix | retired, 2009 | 241-52-0 |
| Jimmy Dorsey | retired, 2008 | 237-78-1 |
| Dale Williams | retired, 1995 | 233-118-3 |
| George Hoblitzell | retired | 232-146-2 |
| Shorty Doyal | deceased | 230-157-6 |
| Jerry Sharp | retired, 2001 | 229-101-9 |
| Bob Sphire | North Gwinnett | 229-73 |
| Rick Tomberlin | Effingham County | 228-105 |
| Rich McWhorter | Charlton County | 227-48-2 |
| Danny Cronic | retired, 2008 | 227-178-1 |
| Jim Walsh | retired, 1994 | 224-111-2 |
| Ed Pilcher | Bainbridge | 223-80-1 |
| Weyman Sellers | retired, 1986 | 223-114-8 |
| Buzz Busby | retired, 2006 | 220-71-3 |
| French Johnson | deceased | 220-110-10 |
| Jeff Herron | Camden County | 219-42-0 |
| Bob Griffith | retired | 219-111-1 |
| Bob Christmas | North Hall | 218-106 |
| Max Bass | retired, 1994 | 217-108-8 |
| Al Reaves | retired, 2000 | 216-160-6 |
| Jim Scroggins | retired, 2009 | 213-136-0 |

# Career Coaching Wins

| Coach | School | Record |
|---|---|---|
| David Dupree | retired, 1983 | 210-79-12 |
| Bob Herndon | retired, 2009 | 210-119-2 |
| Mitt Miller | retired, 2002 | 209-93-0 |
| Jack Johnson | retired, 2004 | 208-79-0 |
| Alton Shell | retired, 1990 | 208-107-2 |
| Bobby Gentry | deceased, 2005 | 204-94-10 |
| Robert Herndon | Benedictine | 204-130-3 |
| Buck Cravey | retired, 1992 | 200-97-10 |
| Rush Propst | Colquitt County | 200-75 |
| Bill Railey | retired, 2004 | 200-73-0 |
| Bill Schofill | retired, 1993 | 200-108-5 |
| Oliver Hunnicut | retired, 1971 | 198-98-19 |
| Max Dowis | retired | 195-202-2 |
| John Mullinax | Armuchee | 195-141 |
| Rayvan Teague | Carrollton | 194-55-1 |
| Mike Earwood | Our Lady of Mercy | 193-85-1 |
| John Peacock | retired, 2002 | 190-105-5 |
| Tom Simonton | retired, 1997 | 188-137-2 |
| Tally Johnson | retired, 2005 | 187-129-8 |
| Bonwell Royal | retired | 187-105-6 |
| Cecil Flowe | Parkview | 186-56 |
| Lynn Hunnicutt | Model | 186-94-1 |
| Bill Thorn | retired, 1998 | 186-84-5 |
| Wayne Parrish | retired | 186-78-0 |
| Charlie Brake | retired, 1972 | 185-54-10 |
| Tom Temple | deceased, 1983 | 184-93-2 |
| Charles Rutland | retired, 2001 | 183-104-6 |
| Dewey Alverson | retired, 1988 | 180-125-5 |
| Ronnie McNeese | retired, 2006 | 179-79-1 |

Courtesy: J. David Patterson, *Georgia High School Football Magazine*

# CREDITS AND COURTESIES

## NEWSPAPERS

*Ashburn Wiregrass Farmer*, December 9, 1965.

*Athens Banner-Herald*. onlineathens.com.

*Atlanta Constitution*.

*Atlanta Journal*.

Cosby, Chip. *Lexington Herald-Leader*, January 13, 2011.

Davis, Will. "A State Championship Remembered: 30 Years Later." *Monroe County Reporter and mymcr.net*, December 8, 2010

*Gainesville Daily News*, December 7, 1952.

*Gainesville Times*, December 22, 1957.

Heeter, Jonathan. *Macon Telegraph*, May 12, 2011.

*Jesup Sentinel*, December 17, 1959.

Lastinger, Mark. *Thomasville Times-Enterprise*, November 18, 2006.

*Lincoln Journal*.

Michaux, Scott. *Augusta Chronicle*, December 20, 2010.

*Rome News-Tribune*.

*Savannah Morning News*.

Shirley, Daniel. *Macon Telegraph*, February 24, 2011.

Snow, Garth. *Augusta Chronicle*, February 7, 2011.

Staats, Wayne. *McDuffie Mirror*, February 10, 2011.

*Thomaston Times*.

Thompson, Clint. *Thomasville Times-Enterprise*, June 14, 2006.

*Valdosta Daily Times*.

Wachter, Jamie. *Thomasville Times-Enterprise*, May 6, 2006.

# WEBSITES

Andrews, Jason. "Desegregation in Coffee County." mgagnon.myweb.uga.edu.
Booker T. Washington High School. BTWBulldogs.com.
Census.gov.
Classicschools.com.
Colquitt County High School. colquitt.k12.ga.us/cchssports.
Facebook.com. "The History of Trojan Football."
Football Friday Night. FootballFridayNight.com.
Georgia High School Association. GHSA.net.
Georgia High School Football Historians Association. GHSFHA.org.
Georgia High School Helmet Project. GaHelmetProject.com.
Georgia National Wrestling Alliance. GNWA.org.
Georgia Public Broadcasting and gpb.org.
GlynnCounty.com.
Hawkinsville High Red Devils. HHSRedDevils.com.
McClendon, Shane. CommerceTigers.com.
Prep Logos. PrepLogos.com.
Prisontalk.com.
Senate Bill 756, March 12, 1998.
Sickler, Scott. LaGrangeFootball.com and Future Star Sports.
Spencer High School. Spencerhighga.org.
Thomasville Bulldogs. TvilleBulldogs.com.
Tiftcountyfootball.com.
John Walton and RedDevils.us.

# BOOKS, MAGAZINES AND PERIODICALS

Asher, Gene. *Legends: Georgians Who Lived Impossible Dreams*. Macon, GA: Mercer University Press, 2005.
*Georgia Trend*.
*In the Game*, April 2011.
Wayne County Friends of the Library. *Wayne County, Georgia: Its History and Its People*. N.p.: Curtis Media Corp, 1990.

# INDIVIDUALS

Jack Hadley at the History Museum in Thomasville.
Tommy Palmer at Palmer Sports Media.
Samcrenshaw.blogspot.com for the Hawkinsville insights.
Maurice Sheppard for the Benedictine-Savannah materials.
Becky Taylor and the GHSBP.
David Waller at the Valdosta Wildcats Museum.

# ABOUT THE AUTHOR

J on Nelson has been a television journalist based in Atlanta for over twenty years. He graduated from Florida State University with a bachelor's of science degree in political science. His television career has given him the opportunity to cover varied events such as Super Bowls, World Series, All-Star Games, Summer Olympiads, the Masters, the U.S. Open, Grey Cups and even political conventions. He has also covered high school athletics for Georgia Public Broadcasting for fifteen years as a host, correspondent and sideline reporter/anchor for the magazine show *SportsCentral* and the GHSA High School Championships.

Visit us at
www.historypress.net